IT'S MY DELIGHT

Beagles on a tiring Jack.

BRIAN VESEY-FITZGERALD

IT'S
MY DELIGHT

Illustrated by
WATKINS-PITCHFORD

LONDON
EYRE & SPOTTISWOODE

First published 1947

Printed in Great Britain for
Eyre & Spottiswoode (Publishers), Limited,
15 Bedford Street, London, W.C.2

CONTENTS

IT'S MY DELIGHT

AUTHOR'S NOTE

This is not a guide book to the bye-ways of Sport. Nor is it a Manual to the Art of Poaching. There is nothing here that the expert does not know, and a great deal the expert does know will not be found here—for obvious reasons. I have done no more than indicate the direction of one or two of the better known by-ways. Those who wish to explore further should follow these signposts. They will find a new and exciting prospect open to them—that there are more things in the English country-side than are dreamt of in the philosophy of the majority of their country-men. Nor is it necessary, or even advisable, to practise in order to explore. Though it is, of course, more thorough.

B. V-F.

Chapter I

THE HARE

The wind's in the east,
  But there's green on the larch,
And a fairy-tale beast
  On the uplands' wide arch
That gallops and gallops, light pacing,
  At chasing
Of Magic, clean Magic of March.
        Patrick Chalmers.

THERE are three sorts of hares in the British Isles—the Brown Hare, the Blue Hare, and the Irish Hare. The Brown Hare occurs in Great Britain wherever there is cultivation, but is rare on moorlands and high up on hills. It has been introduced into Ireland on many occasions without any success. The Blue Hare is common in the Highlands of Scotland above the level of cultivation. Recently it has extended its range south of the Forth, and now appears to be well established there. It has also been introduced with varying success into Northern England, the Snowdonia district of North Wales, and Ireland. The Irish Hare is common in all the mountain districts of the island, and occasionally occurs in considerable numbers on the low ground. It has been introduced, without much success, into Mull, and also into Snowdonia, where it seems to have settled down well.

The Brown Hare (in winter the coat is thicker and a pale, smoky grey) measures between 22 and 24 inches in length, and may weigh anything from 7 to 13 lb., though, exceptionally, animals much in excess of that weight have been recorded. The Blue Hare is smaller. The length is rarely in excess of 20 inches, and the weight varies between 5 and 7 lb., with the heaviest record weighing only

9

$8\frac{1}{2}$ lb. In winter the colour changes to pure white, except for
the ear-tips, which are black. The change is not due to a moult,
but to the action of certain cells which at low temperatures absorb
the colour of the hair. The change, since it matches the colour of
the snow, is protective until the return of the brown coat in the
spring, but it is not an invariable change, and the Blue Hares of
Harris and the Lewis are said never to become really white. The
flesh is much inferior to that of the Brown Hare, and the fur is
woollier and poorer. Brown Hares and Blue Hares will inter-
breed occasionally. The Irish Hare is intermediate in size. The
average length is 23 inches, and the weight varies between 7 and
10 lb. In colour the Irish Hare is redder than the Brown Hare,
but, like the Blue Hare, the coat changes in the winter. It is rare,
however, for the change to be as complete as in the Scottish animal,
for, though pure white animals do occur, it is more usual to find a
russet line along the flanks. There is also a buff variety of the Irish
Hare. The flesh is good—certainly equal to that of the Brown Hare.
There is no proof of breeding with either the Brown or the Blue Hare.

The chief courting season for hares is February and March in
England, and March and April in Scotland. This is the season
when the bucks go " mad "—the March hares of fable. The bucks
run about all day in pursuit of the does, and there is much kicking
and jumping and bucking. The general idea seems to be that
this fighting is confined to the bucks, and I have even read that a
" master " buck will fight off all rivals for his doe. Undoubtedly
the bucks do fight fiercely among themselves, standing up and box-
ing, kicking and so forth. But the does also fight—not each other,
but the bucks—and since they are bigger and more powerfully
built than the bucks, the latter frequently have rather a rough
passage before the union is consummated. Furthermore, there is
no permanent pairing. Hares are promiscuous, and a doe may
be served by two or three bucks in quick succession.

Does begin to breed at about a year old. The period of gestation
is thirty days, and normally there are three or four litters in a year
(they may come in any month of the year), with from two to six
in a litter, though as many as eight have been recorded occasionally.
Young leverets—they are among the most beautiful creatures in
the world—are born covered with hair, open-eyed and able to
run. They are born in the open, and shortly after birth the doe
finds a separate form for each of her young, carries each one to its

form in her mouth (in just the same way as a cat carries her kittens), and thereafter visits them at night to suckle them. Hares are exceptionally good mothers, and will fight fiercely in defence of their young during the period in which the latter are dependant upon them. This is not a long period. At a month old leverets are completely independent.

Brown and Blue Hares are notably solitary and unsocial creatures. The Irish hare, on the other hand, is notably gregarious, and is sometimes seen in companies two or three hundred strong. I do not know about Blue Hares (I have never heard of them being seen in companies), but there seems to have been some change in the habits of the Brown Hare. In Cobbett's day the Brown Hare was either much more common than it is to-day or its habits were rather different. You will remember that Cobbett saw them in great companies on the Wiltshire Downs. Probably they were rather more numerous than they are to-day even in such good hare country as Wiltshire, but I am extremely doubtful if they were so much more plentiful as a casual reading of Cobbett would lead one to believe, for I have myself seen Brown Hares in company in Hampshire, and there have been several reports in *The Field* of Brown Hares in company. No; I think that the Brown Hare has experienced a change of habit. Gathering in companies was common once, and to-day is most uncommon. What the purpose of such occasional gathering may be has not been explained.

Brown Hares prefer low, rolling ground. They spend all their lives in forms in the open. These forms are very carefully selected. They are invariably chosen to give a view—this is the most important factor—but they are also so situated as to give shelter from the prevailing wind, to catch as much sun as possible in winter and as much shade as possible in summer. The Brown Hare spends most of the day in its form. If alarmed in its form it crouches close to the ground, jumping and moving off rapidly when the danger presses. In this way you may know if the object you see in a field is a hare or not. If as you approach the object gets smaller and smaller, it is a hare; if it gets bigger and bigger, it is not. The senses of hearing and smell are very acute, but the sight straight ahead is not at all good, owing to the position of the eyes, though a hare can see well enough anything that is not straight in front of it. The Blue Hare does not make a form. Instead it hides away among stones, or shelters beneath overhanging rocks, and will also use rabbit-holes. (I once bolted a Brown Hare from a rabbit-burrow when ferreting, and I have seen a hunted hare go down a rabbit-burrow. But these were exceptional occurrences.) But, though Blue Hares do not use forms, they separate their young in the same way as the Brown Hare does, visiting them at night to suckle them.

On the whole, hares are silent creatures. A hurt or wounded hare screams—a horribly human sound, like that of a small child that has been hurt, and one that carries for a long way—and courting and fighting hares grunt and hiss. There also seems to be an alarm sound—a clicking, caused, it is said, by grinding the teeth, but of this I cannot speak, for I have never heard it. When the doe is going to suckle her leverets she calls them; a soft, rather feeble bleating that can be heard by humans only at very close range. Does also call to their young to warn them of approaching danger. This is a soft sound that I have heard described as *oont*, but here again I have no personal experience.

Hares do not walk: in fact, they cannot walk. At all speeds, even the slowest, the method of progression is a series of jumps with the hind legs and skips with the fore. Speed is attained by lengthening the jumps. The quicker the pace the farther forward are the footprints of the hind legs in relation to those of the fore. At full speed they are well in front of them. And at full speed the head is outstretched and the ears are laid flat along the back. It has often been said that it is possible to distinguish the sexes of hares by the way in which the animals carry their ears. It has as often been denied. The doe is said always to carry her ears laid flat; the buck to carry one of his partly cocked. Except at full speed I believe this to be true. As might be expected, having regard to its method of progression, the hare is an expert jumper. Jumps of 20 feet and more have often been recorded—one of a full 26 feet has been vouched for—and no hare thinks anything of hopping over a 5-foot fence into a garden. One hare has been watched while clearing a Grand National jump easily.

They are also expert swimmers, both in salt and fresh water. In general, it is probably true to say that they dislike getting their fur wet, and normally, if a hare must cross water, it will go considerably out of its way to cross by a shallow ford or to find a place sufficiently narrow to jump without effort. But there are many exceptions to this general rule. I once knew a hare that had a positive love of water. In the garden of the house in Hampshire in which I was then living there was a shallow pond. It was a made pond, with a concrete bottom, and was nowhere deeper than 18 inches. For several weeks on end during one summer this hare used to come every morning about six o'clock and sit in the water for some five minutes—sitting bolt upright with the ears cocked. It would then get out and shake itself like a dog, move over to the fence, which was 4 feet 6 inches high, jump this without the least effort, and disappear across the fields. I have never heard of another hare taking a morning bath, but the habit may well be fairly common, for some hares will swim without being forced to do so. The classic example of this habit is that given by Yarrell in Louden's *Magazine of Natural History*, Volume V, and since this is now hard to come by, and is, therefore, probably not known to many people, it is worth quoting in full here:

A harbour of great extent on our northern coast has an island near the middle of considerable size, the nearest point of which is a mile distant from the mainland at high water, and with which point there is frequent communication by a ferry. Early one morning in spring two hares were observed to come down from the hills of the mainland towards the seaside; one of which from time to time left its companion and proceeding to the edge of the water, stopped there a moment or two, and then returned to its mate. The tide was rising, and after waiting some time, one of them, exactly at high water, took to the sea and swam rapidly over, in a straight line, to the opposite point of land. The observer on this occasion, who was near the spot but remained unobserved by the hares, had no doubt that they were of different sexes, and that it was the male that swam across the water, as he had probably done many times before. It was remarkable that the hares had remained on the shore nearly half an hour; one of them occasionally examining, as it would seem, the state of the current, and ultimately taking to the sea at that precise period of the tide called slack water, when the passage across could be effected without being carried by the force of the stream either above or below the desired point of landing. The other hare then cantered back to the hills.

There have been many other instances of hares swimming in the sea, and several of hares taking to the sea when hunted. And of hares swimming in fresh water, crossing rivers, lakes and so on, there have been innumerable instances. One recorded by E. H. in *Nature* (Vol. XXXIX, p. 306) may be taken as typical:

I was by the little river Arun below the old mill at Pulborough one day, when I saw a hare quietly cantering down the opposite field towards the river. A bank hid the actual crossing from me; but when the hare emerged from the water into the field in which I was standing, I was amused to see the dog-like fashion in which it stood and shook off the moisture, scattering the spray far and wide before resuming its leisurely canter. The act had the air of being habitual.

I have myself seen hares swimming the Itchen on five occasions, and I once saw one pursued by the beagles, and hard pressed at that, plunge into the canal near Wilcot in Wiltshire, swim across, and make good its escape. The hares entering the water to cross the Itchen did so very gently, and took care not to wet their heads. All five crossings were made at about the same place and had the appearance of being habitual. The hunted hare plunged in with a considerable splash, disappeared entirely for a moment, and then came to the surface swimming strongly. Once on the other bank it made off without stopping to shake itself. All the Itchen hares stopped to shake themselves just as described by the writer in *Nature*.

As they do not burrow, and as they are in themselves cleanly animals, hares do not do so much damage as rabbits. But they are very destructive all the same, and in so small and over-populated a country as our own are very much too common. They are wholly vegetarian, and eat chiefly grasses and roots, and can and do do a great deal of damage to growing crops, especially young corn, mangolds, turnips, and swedes. But they have also two favourite and little-known foods: fungi and the sea-pea, the latter, of course, known only to those hares that live near the sea-beaches. The late Charles Cornish, a charming and accurate writer on country matters who is not so widely known to-day as he ought to be, writing in the *Country Life* volume on *Shooting*, says:

A curious fact in hare life is their exceeding fondness for sea-beaches, especially those on which certain sea-plants grow. The favourite plant of all is a somewhat rare one, the sea-pea (*Lathyrus maritima*), which grows on the shingles, and especially on the pebble banks like that at Orford (which is nine miles long) and on the Chesil beach, and on others in Sussex and Devon. This pea sends down its roots many feet into the shingles, and spreads like a mat of dark-green salty leaves over yards of stones. On Chesil beach the hares come down from the hills to eat this plant, and below Orford they actually swim the broad tidal river to get it. Thence they travel down the beach, and so reach the mainland near Alde-burgh. The only vegetation is a thin dry grass in places, and the sea-campion. Yet forty hares may be shot in a day, and often are, on this hard bed of stones, in excellent condition.

They are also very fond of fungi, especially the mushroom, the various puff-balls, Scotch bonnets, Shaggy Ink Caps, and several others. They will invade gardens to get at morels, which often grow in borders. Unlike the rabbit, when eating turnips, hares tear down and leave the outside, and when eating wheat they leave the ears and take the stalks and leaves. The damage they can do in a field of grain has to be seen to be believed. And in a garden they can wreak havoc. In the kitchen-garden they seem to prefer carrots, lettuces, parsley, and broccoli. By that, I mean that if those plants are present (as they almost always are) they will take them in preference to others, but if they are not, they will take what is. In the flower-garden they seem to be especially fond of wallflowers and carnations and primulas. But again, do not think that by not grow-ing these plants you will avoid visits from hares. In my experience almost any other plant will suit the hare just as well. And the hare is a very difficult animal to keep out of a garden if it wants to come in. Few fences are high enough to stop it, and few gates can be kept permanently shut. Fortunately the hare is an exceptionally easy animal to snare. There are two other interesting points about the feeding habits of the hare. Part of the food passing from the bowel is immediately re-swallowed and passed again. And hares will not graze grass that has been defiled by rabbits.

It is the common belief that the hare is an excessively timid animal. I do not think that it is. A doe will fight fiercely in defence of its young. It will drive off cattle from its form. It is more than a match for a small terrier, and can deliver a very telling blow with its hind legs. It is altogether a strong, even a powerful, animal. I have had a full-grown wild hare in my arms, and though I am by no means a small man, I had all my work cut out to get it under control, and was severely scratched and bitten. So far from being timid, I believe that the hare has supreme confidence in its own powers, and especially in its speed, and I agree whole-heartedly with Mr. C. B. Shepherd that it has also a queer sense of humour. Mr. Shepherd, in his contribution to the Lonsdale

Library volume on Beagling, gives several instances in support of this, and I have myself watched a hare deliberately leading a fox a dance and obviously enjoying doing so.

Richard Blome in *The Gentleman's Recreation*, which was published in 1686, says: "There are four sorts of Hares. Some live in mountains, some in the fields, some in the marshes, some everywhere without any certain place of abode. They of the mountains are the most swift, they of the fields less nimble, they of the marshes most slow, and the wandering hares are the most dangerous to follow, for they are so cunning in their ways and muses of the fields, running up the hills and rocks because by custom they know the nearer way, with other tricks, to the confusion of the dogs, and the discouragement of the hunters." And he goes on: "It is admirable to behold how every limb and member of this beast is composed for celerity." And again: "Though their sight be dim, yet they have an indefatigable Sense of Seeing, so that the continuance in a mean degree, countervaileth in them the want of excellence." Richard Blome, of course, was writing from the hunting point of view, and from that point of view his words are as sound to-day as the day they were written, provided you do not take "mountains" literally. By "mountains" Blome meant "downs"—and you will remember that no less a man than Gilbert White of Selborne also called the South Downs mountains. With this reservation kept in mind, Blome was perfectly correct in his estimation of hares. The Blue Hare of the mountains is, comparatively, a slow animal, but the Brown Hare of the downland is an animal of immense speed, infinitely faster than, say, his cousin of the Kentish marshlands. Indeed, from the point of view of hunting, woodland hares and marshland hares provide the worst sport. They seem to be altogether softer, less speedy, and less resourceful than their cousins of the hills and open fields, and they rarely stand up before hounds for any length of time.

Leverets, as I have already said, are born fully clothed, open-eyed and able to run if need be. But they do not run if they can possibly help it. They much prefer to lie in the form chosen for them by their mother, and they lie so close that it requires a very keen eye to spot them. They will continue to lie so until the very last moment, and, indeed, beyond that moment, for it is possible to pick them up before they can make up their minds to move. I have done so more than once. The doe does not live in the midst of the nursery of forms she has chosen for her young, but in separate form a little distance away. And she visits them only a night for the purpose of suckling them. But she is never too far away to be of help in giving warning of approaching danger or to help in driving away feeding cattle. She continues to feed them for about three weeks or a month, after which they fend for themselves. But for about two months after the mother has left them to their own devices young hares prefer to lie low in their forms and to adventure cautiously into the outside world, and then only at twilight. Though they have considerable speed, they are disinclined to trust it. And in this they are wise, for, though they are fast enough, they cannot maintain speed for any distance. Young hares lack stamina and tire very easily.

Does seem to pass the whole of their lives in the same district. I do not think that this can truly be said of bucks. Possibly bucks have a sort of headquarters in the district in which they were born—many authorities maintain that this is the case—and wander only in the search for females, but I am inclined to think that the bucks are wanderers always. Certainly they keep to a form for a shorter space of time than do the does. On an average, provided that she is not unduly disturbed, a doe will keep to the same form for some three weeks. She will then leave it for another in the immediate vicinity, and probably throughout the year she will not have more than four or five forms on which she will ring the changes. By that I do not mean that the form remains as a form until she comes back into residence again—obviously that is not so—but that she has four or five spots in which she makes her form during the course of a year. This is definitely not the case with the buck. I do not believe that a buck keeps to a form for more than a fortnight at a time, and I do not believe that a buck rings the changes on a number of favourite situations in the course of a year.

Hares are very easily tamed if caught young enough. They are, however, animals of character and strong individualists, which accounts for the very different stories of tame hares one hears. And no doubt a great deal depends on the amount of trouble taken over their education. Every one interested in hares or in poetry knows the story of the poet Cowper's hares. He had one which he kept for ten years, and about which he wrote these lines:

" Leverets . . . are born fully clothed."

The surliest of his kind,
    Who, nursed with tender care,
And to domestic bounds confined,
    Was still a wild jack hare.

Though duly from my hand he took
    His pittance every night,
He did it with a jealous look,
    And, when he could, would bite.

Others have had similar experience. V. T., writing in *The Field* in 1902 (this account is also quoted by Mr. Eric Parker in his Lonsdale Library volume), says of two leverets brought to him by a keeper:

> I put them into a low, wide tin bath, wired all around and over the top. They were at first terrified, and sat huddled together for the remainder of the day and night, refusing food of any sort. In the early hours of the morning I succeeded in feeding them with some warm milk—and again later—till, by degrees, they began to nibble clover. I tamed them by slow stages, till they would eat from my hand and let me nurse them. But as their fear of me gradually diminished I was amazed to find how forcibly and persistently they were prepared to resent interference. They flew at me, bit and scratched me, making a most peculiar hissing sound, and so ferocious and hurtful were their attacks that I was forced to defend myself with a pair of thick gloves. . . . Then followed a series of boxing matches, the assaults upon me frequently lasting several minutes, with periodical rests, when they would retire to a corner, regain their wind, and attack me again more savagely than before. When completely beaten, they would let me stroke them and lick my hand as usual, and be friends again.

But they grew up. V. T. continues:

> One of these hares is now a most engaging animal, knows me perfectly, and will jump up on my knee, climb up and kiss me when told, sit up and beg, jump through a hoop, and shake hands, always giving me the right paw. It will also seek its food when I hide it, and does all in its power to show its affection for me. It lives in the house, is loose all day, and thoroughly enjoys a good roll on the rug, where it frequently lies stretched full length before the fire. It also plays with two retriever dogs, of whom it has no fear whatever, and often lies between them when asleep.

Hares when kept in captivity will usually make friends with the dogs of the household, and show no fear of them, and the dogs, in my experience, like the hares and become very attached to them. I knew a Cairn Terrier that never got over the death of its hare companion, and moped so badly, refusing food and comfort of any sort, that finally it had to be put away. Cats also take kindly to hares for company in the house. One I knew of used always to bring her kittens shortly after birth and place them in the big basket that the hare lived in, and the hare would curl herself around them and mother them in the most engaging fashion while the real mother was about the many businesses of a grown cat, but would immediately relinquish her place when the cat returned.

Hares are said never to drink. I must say that I have never seen a wild hare drink, and I have never heard of any one who has. But I have seen a tame hare drink, and enjoy drinking so much that I cannot believe it was a totally new habit. This hare was the property of a notorious old poacher, and was petted and cosseted as if it were an only child. Every evening it would accompany its master down to the " local " and take up a position on the counter of the bar. The old man would order a pint of mild and bitter for himself and a saucer of mild for the hare. And the hare would drink this just as a cat drinks, which is different from the way a dog drinks. Of course, the visitors to the bar always wanted to stand the hare another, but the old man would not allow this, though he was by no means averse to being stood another, and more, himself. Having seen that his pet had had her evening drink, and having got all he could himself, he would leave for the more serious business of the evening, followed by the hare. This would lollop along at his heels just like a dog all the way back to his cottage, and no village dog ever set upon it. Indeed, there were not wanting those who maintained that the old man took it out with him on his poaching expeditions. There were not wanting those who went even farther than that, and credited the animal with superhuman powers.

There must be something about the hare, for there is nothing new in this belief about its connection with superhuman powers. The hare has always been deeply involved in our folk-lore and witch-lore. In the Isle of Man, even to this day, it is regarded as the favourite form of a witch, and no pure Manxman would dream of eating a hare. That is true even to-day in the parts of the island that have not been too overrun by the tourist traffic, but whereas not so many years ago the people would admit that they would not dream of eating a hare, to-day they will not admit anything so foolish; they just do not eat hares. This belief that witches change into hares at night is not confined to the Isle of Man. It was once common all over England, and it is by no means dead yet, any more than black magic is dead. In Christina Hole's *English Folklore* there is mention of the witch of Winterslow. Her name was Lyddie Shears, and she lived at the beginning of the last century. Not only could she turn herself into a hare, but she had power over hares, and poachers used to give her presents to find the creatures for them. She would go on to the Downs and strike lights from a flint, and the hares would spring up on all sides, and the poachers would kill them while they were still dazzled by the flashes. She was eventually shot by a silver bullet while running as a hare, and was found dead in her cottage with the bullet in her heart. Shooting with a silver bullet is the traditional way of dealing with witches, and there are many similar stories. In fact, I heard of one for this century from Dorset not so long ago. Belief in the presence of witches has not died out, and the hare is still regarded in some parts of the country as the home at night of elderly women of doubtful powers. There is a village near Ilminster that is popularly supposed by neighbours to hold witches; there is another in Hampshire; another in Dorset; several in Ireland.

A magical animal, the hare: an animal around which all sorts of legends have gathered. Pliny mentions the fable that " hares are of many and various sexes ". Sir Thomas Browne did not go as far as that. He limited the sexes to two, but he believed that they were inter-changeable, and in his *Inquiries into Common and Vulgar Errors* he tells us that the buck will occasionally give birth to young. And in some of the oldest Welsh laws it is expressly stated that the hare is outside legal valuation, since in one month it is a female and in the next a male. Thomas Pennant, too, who made a tour of Wales in the latter part of the eighteenth century, tells us that in Montgomery hares were known as St. Monacella's lambs. " When a hare was pursued by dogs it was believed that if any one cried ' God and St. Monacella be with thee ' it was sure to escape."

A magical animal then. And still an animal filled with magic.

Chapter II

TO HUNT THE HARE

*I like the hunting of the hare
Better than that of the fox.*

Wilfrid Scawen Blunt.

HARE-HUNTING is very much older than fox-hunting. It is so old that its earlier history is lost in the mists of antiquity. Xenophon, who lived from 435 to 354 B.C., cheered his hounds on the slopes of Mount Pholoe, and we may be sure that—and this from his own writings, for he describes in detail in his *Cyneticus* the methods then in vogue for this kind of hunting—he was not the first to cheer hounds in pursuit of the hare. And we know that Xenophon's hounds were scenting-hounds, for we are told by Arrian that the greyhound was unknown in the days of the great Greek general and historian. We have no need to go farther back: Xenophon provides an ancient and respectable enough pedigree for the sport of hunting the hare. And despite the strange predilection of the Norman Kings for the sport of hunting the deer, the hare was for many centuries regarded as the finer quarry of the two. Edward, Duke of York, himself one of the greatest of all writers on sport, in his book *The Master of Game* gives the hare precedence over the hart. He says—and who shall gainsay him?— "It is to be known that the hare is king of all venery, for all blowing and the fair terms of hunting cometh of the seeking and the finding of the hare. For certain it is the most marvellous beast that is."

And having started with *The Master of Game* let me continue. The author has this to say on the proper hunting of the hare:

> It is a fair thing to slay her with strength of hounds, for she runneth strong and cunningly. A hare shall last well four miles or more or less, if she be an old male hare.

And when at last she fails and "is bitten by hounds":

> Whoso is nearest should take her whole from them, and hold her in his one hand over his head high, and blow the death that men may gather thither, and when they be come, then should she be stripped, all save the head, and the gall and the paunch cast away, and the remnant should be laid on a great staff or on a board, whoso hath it, or on the earth, and then it should be chopped as small as it can be, so that it hangs together; and when it is so done then should one of the berners take it up with the head and hold it as high as he is able in his hands, and then whoso is the most master, blow the death, and anon as he beginneth every man help and holloa. And when the hounds have bayed as long as is wished by the aforesaid most master, then should the berner pull as high as he can every piece from the other and cast to every hound his reward. And then should the most master blow a mote and a stroke, if so be that he thinks that the hounds have done enough, and else he should rest awhile, if the hounds be hot, till they be cooled, and then led to the water to lap. And then if he wish blow three motes and uncouple and speak and so do as before said.

Such was hare-hunting in the fourteenth century. The sport then differed in many ways from the sport as we know it to-day, though not so widely as it differed from the sport as Xenophon knew it. Hounds, for example, must have been much faster than the Greek hounds that hunted the hares of Mount Pholoe, and maybe were not so very much slower than the hounds of the sixteenth century, though very much slower than the hounds of to-day. In Xenophon's time the hounds must have been very slow indeed, for the method of catching the hare was by means of nets placed across the runs which the huntsman thought the most likely to be used by the hare. It was very rarely that the hounds actually caught a hare themselves. The idea was to keep the hare on the move, so that finally she might run into one of the nets that the huntsman had placed. The hunting was really a test of the wood-craft of the huntsman rather than a test of hounds. If the nets had vanished by the time of Edward, Duke of York—and his work was largely a transcription of an earlier work by Count Gaston de Foix, called *La Chasse*, which is commonly known as *Gaston Phoebus*—the work of the hounds was still very slow by modern standards. But, then, so was life. There was not so much to do, and there was a great deal more time in which to do it. Our forebears went about life in a much more deliberate manner. They used to start hunting at a very early hour, and they used to start by hunting the trace the hare had left during her feeding the previous night, unravelling it as they went along, until finally they put her up from her form. Then the hunt proper began, and frequently it was a pretty long one. There is an account of a day with the harriers of Sir Roger de Coverley, at the end of which the hare is said to have been picked up alive eight yards in front of the hounds, who had been hunting her for nearly as many hours. That is evidence enough of the slowness of the pace. Had there been any sort of a pace, no hare could have been alive at the end of such a day. Nowadays, too frequently, the merit of a hunt is judged by the number of minutes without a check; then it was judged by the amount of sport a hare could give, and the longer after the hare was found the better. In *Of the Hunting of an Hare* it is impressed upon the huntsman that he should mark carefully the first runs and circles of the hare, for " she will all day long hold the same wayes ". One hare; all day long. Life was indeed leisurely in those days.

Hunting the hare was the principal sport of the majority of country squires and farmers during the sixteenth century, and for the greater part of the seventeenth also, and it had, possibly, become widely popular during the latter half of the fifteenth century. Probably most country squires and some yeoman farmers kept a few couple of hounds with which they hunted whenever they felt inclined. Indeed, it seems likely that there are very few villages in England and Wales that have not at some time had their pack of hounds. What were these hounds like? It can be taken that there was little uniformity over the country as a whole before the end of the sixteenth century, but from then onwards the sport began to grow outwards from the small private pack, began to burst its parish boundaries, and certain types began to predominate. We do know something of this early progression from two of the greatest figures in our hunting literature, William Somervile and Peter Beckford. William Somervile, author of *The Chase*, which

" To hunt the hare."

remains the greatest poem in the literature of the sport, lived from 1677 to 1742, and kept hounds for hunting the hare at Edstone near Stratford-on-Avon. Peter Beckford, author of *Thoughts on Hunting*, which he wrote in 1779, and which remains the classic prose work in the literature of the sport, lived from 1740 to 1809, and kept hounds for hare-hunting at Steepleton-Iwerne in Dorset.

William Somervile kept two small packs. You will remember his lines in *The Chase*:

> A different hound, for every diff'rent chase,
> Select with judgement; nor the timorous hare
> O'ermatched destroy, but leave that vile offence
> To the mean, murd'rous, coursing crew, intent
> On blood and spoil. Oh blast their hopes, just Heaven!

It was the custom at that time for country squires and yeoman farmers owning small packs to hunt buck, fox, and hare indiscriminately with the same hounds. Somervile practised what he preached and kept two packs; about twelve couple of foxhounds, "rather rough and wire-haired," with which he hunted the fox and an occasional buck, and some of which he used for hunting the otter in the summer; and about twelve couple of harriers, which were bred between the old Cotswold hound (a small hound, almost a beagle) and the old Southern hound, and which he kept solely for hare-hunting.

For Peter Beckford's hare-hounds I cannot do better than quote his own description:

> The hounds, I think, most likely to show you sport, are between the large slow-hunting harrier and the little fox beagle: one is too dull, too heavy, and too slow; the other, too lively, too light, and too fleet. The first, it is true, have most excellent noses, and I make no doubt will kill their game at last, if the day be long enough; but you know the days are short in winter, and it is bad hunting in the dark. The others, on the contrary, fling and dash, and are all alive; but every cold blast affects them; and if your country is deep and wet, it is not impossible but some of them may be drowned. My hounds were a cross of both these kinds, in which it was my endeavour to get as much bone and strength in as small a compass as possible. It was a difficult undertaking. I bred many years, and an infinity of hounds before I could get what I wanted: I, at last, had the pleasure to see them very handsome; small, yet very bony: they ran remarkably well together; ran fast

enough; had all the alacrity you could desire; and would hunt the coldest scent. When they were thus perfect, I did as many others do—I parted with them.

Peter Beckford's hounds, or rather harriers, were obviously bred on much the same lines as William Somervile's, for both sprang from crosses between the same two types of hare-hounds, commonly in vogue with the squires of the west and south-west. But these were not the only sorts of hounds in the country at the time. In *An Essay on Hunting*, published in 1733 (and who wrote it, I wonder?), there occurs the following:

> The Hounds most in use and proper for Hare-hunting, may be confined to few sorts, and each excellent in nature: to wit, the deep-tongued, thick-lipped, broad and long-hung southern Hounds.
> The fleet sharp-nosed Dog, ears narrow and pointed, deep chested, with thin shoulders, portending a quarter of the Fox-strain.
> The rough wire-haired Hound, thick-quartered, well hung, not too fleshy shouldered, together with the rough or smooth Beagle.
> Each of these sorts, as I said before, have their excellencies, etc. It is not possible, with justice, to commend one before another, for kind, colour, or service, preference being given according to the humours and inclinations of Sportsmen, the tribe of whom are very numerous, and, of consequence, different in opinion.
> He that delights in a long chace of six hours, often more, and to be in with the dogs all the time, let him breed of the southern Hounds first mentioned, or such heavy Dogs as Sussex Gentlemen run in the weald. They make good deep bass musick, afford great diversion, and, considering how dirty the country is (notwithstanding a hunt often lasts all day long), fatigue the healthy footman very little.
> In an open country where there is good riding, prefer the second sort, with a quarter of Fox-strain: these suit the more eager, active Horseman, and spend their tongues generously, making delightful harmony, and at the same time go at such a rate, a hare durst not play many tricks before them; they seldom allow her time to loiter; she must run and continue her foiling or change soil, if the latter she dies: keep in, Huntsman; fresh ground on the turf is in some degree a continued view, otherwise hang your Dogs, (barring extraordinary accidents of highways and sheep blemish) for I would no more excuse the loss of a Hare on fresh sward, unless the Huntsman's fault, which is too often the case, than I would a kennel of Fox-hounds losing Reynard in full chace; the reasons against it in both diversions are the same.
> The slow Hounds mentioned generally pack best. Of the second

sort, many not being of equal speed, (for it is hard to procure an even kennel of fast Hounds) will be found to tail, which is an inconveniency; for the hind Dogs labour on to overtake the leading Hounds, and seldom or ever stop, nor are of the least use but to enlarge the cry, unless at an over-run, which happens at the top of the morn, for a quarter of a mile together; then the old Hounds, thrown out or tailed, often come up, and hit the fault off.

The southern Dogs are not so guilty of running a-head; for as they pack well together, from their equality of speed, (it being easier to excel the slow than the fast,) at the least balk there are ten noses on the ground for one.

The third species of Hounds mentioned I never saw an entire kennel of, being in some parts not much encouraged: they are of northern breed, and in great esteem, being bold Dogs, and by many Huntsmen preferred for Otter and Martin: in some places they are encouraged for Fox-hounds, but bad to breed from, being too subject to degenerate and produce thick, low, heavy shouldered Dogs unfit for the chace.

Beagles, rough or smooth, have their admirers; they spend their tongues free in treble or tenor, and go a greater rate than the southern Hounds, but tail abominably. They run low to ground, therefore enjoy the scent better than taller Dogs, especially when the atmosphere lies low. In an enclosed country they do best, as they muse with the Hare, and at trailing or default, are pretty good for hedgerows; yet I have seen eighty couple in the field, out of which, in a winter's sport, I observed not four couple that could be depended on, the majority being so propense to challenge feather or flesh; yet by the assistance of a clever Huntsman, and foil well trod, I have sometimes seen pretty diversion.

Of the two sorts I prefer the rough, or wire-haired, being generally good shouldered Dogs, and well-filleted.

Smooth-haired Beagles are commonly deep hung, thick lipped, and large nostrilled, but, often so soft, solid, and bad quartered, as to be shoulder-shook and crippled the first season's hunt, and have frequently that unpardonable fault of crook legs, like the Tarrier, or Right Bath Turnspit.

I know admirers of this sort, but they are no favourites of mine; few will ensure a tolerable hunt, or at default bear hard charging. After two hours running, observe them crippled and down; the Huntsman may go on himself, for what assistance many of them give him; and it is plain from their form and shape (for nature makes nothing in vain) that they are not designed for hard exercise.

Peter Beckford's little " fox-beagle " does not appear to be in the above description, but I think that it was probably the " fleet sharp-nosed Dog ", or a smaller edition of it, for in fact the author's breeds fall into two sharp divisions—harriers and beagles, and the latter no more than smaller editions of two of the harriers.

There were, then, in the eighteenth century three distinct types of harriers and two types of beagles. To-day there are still three distinct types of harriers, but the beagles have become standardised into one type, beyond all doubt a great improvement on anything that Beckford knew. Our modern harriers are no doubt rather different from the harriers of the eighteenth century, but the difference is not so great that the descent cannot be seen clearly.

The old Southern hound is still to be found occasionally in a few of the harrier kennels, notably, perhaps, in the Holcombe Harriers. The wire-haired hound has disappeared as a hare-hunting hound, but the blood is certainly dead in this country. It is to be found in the modern otter-hound and I think probably in the Welsh fox-hound; but it is not beyond the bounds of possibility that a little of the blood exists in our modern third strain of harrier—the West-country hound, that is lemon or badger-pied. This is usually regarded as a new breed, and it is usually said that it is at least partly descended from the old-fashioned staghound. That there is staghound blood in the breed is certainly true, but I fancy that some of the old harrier may be there also. The old type that has certainly disappeared as a hare-hunting hound is the fast galloper with a " quarter fox-strain ". This has become a foxhound, albeit a small foxhound. And we have now an entirely new breed (new to this country, that is) hunting the hare; and that is the Basset.

Of the three types of harrier still to be found in this country, the oldest is undoubtedly that which now hunts the Holcombe country. The Holcombe Harriers are a very old pack, and they have kept fairly true to the old type of hound : that is, the old Southern hound. And, curiously, the Southern hound during the eighteenth century, and probably well into the nineteenth, was really at home in the north, though it, or a very similar type, was in use in the weald of Sussex. The name Southern had, of course, nothing to do with the south of England. It was not known as the Southern hound in Lancashire because it came from Sussex, but because it came originally from France, as did all our hounds.

In the *Sportsman's Cabinet* there is this description of the Southern hound :

This hound, formerly so very highly estimated, is readily distinguished by his superior size, great strength and majestic solemnity of appearance; in the body he is long, in the carcase round, chest deep, ears long and sweeping, with a tone in the cry, peculiarly deep, mellow and attracting. From the particular formation of the olfactory organs, or from the extra secretion of glandular moisture, which always adheres to the nose and lips, or to some other latent cause, it is endued with the most exquisite sense of smelling, and often distinguishes the scent an hour after the lighter beagles have given it up: their slowness affords them opportunity to receive the assistance and instructions of the huntsman, in a much greater degree than those of a fleeter description; but as they are so well enabled to hunt a cold scent, they are too apt to make it so, by their tardiness in action, and too minute exactness.

These hounds were once universally known, and equally common in every part of the kingdom, and the breed were then cultivated much larger than those now to be found in the low and marshy parts of the country, where they are still in use for the purposes of the chase; although it has been said, " that the breed which has been gradually declining, and its size studiously diminished by a mixture of both kinds, in order to increase speed, is now almost extinct ".   The assertion of this author, however, savours much more of speculative conjecture than of experimental practice; for the present writer hunted the winter of 1775, in the neighbourhood of Manchester, with each of the two packs supported by subscription in that town: one of which was denominated the southern-hounds (uniform of the subscribers, blue, with white cuffs and capes), the other called the beagles; the uniform, scarlet, with silver buttons and green velvet capes. The southern (or old English-hound) is, most undoubtedly, the original real-bred harrier of this country, and most particularly in those swampy parts where the chase is wished to be protracted, without prolonging the distance. The Reverend editor of *Rural Sports* corroborates the above remark of the southern hounds being adapted to the low, marshy, and moory countries by saying, he once saw, at Mr. Wild's, in Lancashire, a numerous pack of hounds kept to hunt hare, the least of which stood *twenty-two inches*, and the huntsman went with *a pole on foot;* and true this is, for in some of the peat-moors and coal-pits in the environs of Manchester, and its surrounding neighbourhood, no horseman whatever, however well mounted, would be able to go with the hounds.

These hounds of Lancashire, and especially those of Mr. Wild, were in all probability the ancestors of the modern Holcombe Harriers, which still hunt in Lancashire, and have been kennelled at Holcombe for more than two hundred years.

But the Southern hound was not only in Lancashire, though that was the county where it was best known, for Blaine, in his *Rural Sports*, says:

> The old Southern hound . . . was formerly strong and large, with a monstrous head, overhanging chaps, full in the throat and dew lapped. This dog is now rarely met with; but a somewhat lengthened type is occasionally seen, and they still preserve the general characters. In colour the Southern hound is mottled, pied or liver coloured, and sometimes nearly black, but in such cases the tintings are elegantly relieved with tan markings. . . . Until within thirty or forty years, the heavy deep-flewed Southern hound was to be met with in several inclosed and deeply earthed counties. As irrigation drained the lands, and cultivation improved the soil, and enabled the sportsman to follow the chase on horseback, a lighter breed was employed. But even within a very few years, the Weald of Sussex was hunted by these slow hounds, whose bass music raised the echo around, and made the welkin ring. The want of speed in this dog is admirably compensated for by his unerring nose and his determined perseverance, which thus makes the trial between the pursuers and the pursued on an equality, and also enables the followers to become witnesses of every stratagem of the hare, and every hit of the dogs. The general *rush* to the head, which would delight the modern hare hunter, would have distanced the olden one, even had he been mounted on the stately palfrey, or the domestic pad.
>
> The old Sussex blue mottled harriers, which formed perhaps the first step in the fining of the original stock, are now nearly extinct, and only to be met with in the weald of that county, some heavy parts of Kent, and a few other vicinities.

These Sussex hounds were the ancestors of the Hailsham Harriers. The Hailsham were given up about 1920, and their place was taken by the Rother Valley Harriers. I do not know if the old blood still survives. Sir John Buchanan-Jardine suggests that it does still linger in a few individuals, but the last time that I saw the Rother Valley I could not see any sign of the blue mottled type. The Hailsham used to show some wonderful sport to followers on foot, and it will be a great pity if the blood disappears altogether. However, you do occasionally see a blue mottled hound in Sussex even to-day.

The modern harrier is often of pure foxhound blood, and what is known to-day as a harrier (without any prefix) has always a proportion of foxhound blood. There is nothing new in this. Foxhound blood has been used for hare-hunting for a very long time. " Nimrod ", writing in 1840, says:

The modern harrier bears no greater resemblance to the one in use fifty years back, than the hunter of the present to that ridden by our grandfathers.   In fact, he is now nothing less than the fox-hound in miniature, which it is the endeavour of all breeders to have him.   Their qualities also are as opposite as their form, the one delighting to dwell upon the scent, the other a little inclined, perhaps, to the other extreme.   But the taste of the day for all sports of the field would not endure the tedious exactness of the old psalm-singing harrier; and not only in point of diversion, but on the score of the " pot ", the balance is greatly in favour of the improved variety.   Before the old-fashioned harrier, the hare had time to play all sorts of tricks, to double on her foil, and so stain the ground that she often escaped by such means; whereas the modern hound, if the scent be tolerably good, forces her from her foil to fly the country, and very often beyond her knowledge, when a good straightforward run is the almost invariable result.   The observation of Mr. Beckford holds good here.   He could not, he said, imagine a hound too well bred to show sport, and kill his game; but he could readily conceive the reverse, when the game ran stout and well.

To Sir John Dashwood King, Bart., of West Wycombe Park, Bucks, is the credit due for what may be termed the living model of the present improved harrier; and so characteristically stamped are his sort of hound, now widely spread, that they are recognised by a sportsman at the first glance.   Their standard height does not exceed eighteen inches, and, therefore, in that respect, they were not an overmatch for their game; but from the great equality of their size and speed, combined with rare hunting qualities, they killed more hares, with good runs, than any other pack in the kingdom, and for many, many years in succession certainly " bore the bell ".   Sir John kept them more than thirty years, at Bourton-on-the-Hill, Gloucestershire, near the four-shire stone on the Oxford and Worcester road, where his father kept them before him; hunting partly in the vales of Warwickshire and Worcester-shire, and partly over the Cotswold Hills, which latter country is famous for the stoutness of its hares, frequently standing an hour before this celebrated pack, after having been driven beyond their knowledge by their pressing method of hunting up to them, a method quite unpractised by the old long-eared harrier.

There is a good deal of difference of opinion as to the right conformation for the modern harrier.   Naturally, perhaps, since a good deal must depend on the country over which the pack hunts. The general run of modern harriers is from 18 to 21 inches in height, though I have lately seen a number of 22.   Personally I think that 20 inches is quite tall enough, and I like to see harriers of less than that height. There is, I understand, a great deal of difficulty in breeding harriers of level size, but I do not know why this should be so. It should surely be as possible to fix the type and size of a harrier as of any other breed. And it certainly should be possible with a breed so scientifically studied as the foxhound, and the modern harrier is no more than a miniature foxhound. Again, it has been my experience that the lighter-built hounds are the best from the stamina point of view; they seem to last the longest and to do the most work in a season. And, again in my experience (and this is heresy, or something very near it), those with " hare-feet " seem to do better than those without, especially on heavy country. It is the aim of every breeder to breed out " hare-feet ". I often wonder if this is wise? By nature dogs were intended to have a long knee-joint. Length in this joint gives elasticity, and so saves a jar to the shoulder when landing from a jump. I believe that the modern craze for a short joint—and it is a craze—is wrong and that we shall pay for it in the long run.

The Western, or West Country, Harrier is a quite distinct breed. It is said, on the authority of Parson Jack Russell, to be descended from the old staghound, and he describes the breed of the early nineteenth century as being light in colour, having plenty of tongue, and being full of drive. Speaking of the Rev. John Froude's pack, he said that he had never seen a better or more killing pack in all his life; high praise indeed from such a man. Froude, who was the Vicar of Knowstone, in North Devon, was probably the founder of the Western Harrier as a distinct breed, and his pack became so famous that the blood was in great demand throughout Devonshire. His hounds were white marked with a little grey and stood about 21 inches high. The modern Western is not so very different from Froude's prototype, and I imagine that should the Reverend gentleman by any chance be able to return for a short visit to the West Country, he would recognise the strain immediately. The colour has altered little, if at all, but the size has come down a little, and the best of the modern Western Harriers do not stand much over 18 inches in height. And their cry is lovely.

The beagle is a breed of great antiquity. It was widely known in the time of Henry VII, and that means that it must have been well established long before that. The origin of the breed is not

c

known, but it seems likely that it originated as a miniature of larger breeds. The rough-haired beagle was probably a miniature of the old Welsh hound, and the smooth-haired of the old southern hound. Though so widely known by early Tudor times and onwards through the seventeenth and early eighteenth centuries, beagles by the end of the eighteenth century had fallen on bad days. In the *Sportsman's Cabinet*, which was published in 1804, will be found the following:

> Previous to the present improved state of hunting, and polish of field sports, packs of beagles were frequently seen in the possession of gentlemen whose age or infirmities prevented their enjoyment of sport of a different description; but in proportion to the gradational improvements made in the different kinds of hounds (according to the different chases they were intended to pursue), the former attachment to beagles has been observed to decline. They are the smallest of the hound race used in this country, are exquisite in their scent of the hare, and indefatigably vigilant in their pursuit of her. Though wonderfully inferior in point of speed, yet equally energetic in persevering pursuit, they follow her through all her windings, unravel all her mazes, explore her labyrinths, and by the scent alone trace, and retrace her footsteps to a degree of admiration that must be seen to be properly understood; during all which the soft and melodious tone of their emulous vociferation seems to be the most predominant inducement to the well-known ecstatic pleasures of the chase.
>
> This slow kind of hunting was admirably adapted to age and the feminine gender; it could be enjoyed by ladies of the greatest timidity as well as gentlemen labouring under infirmity; to both of whom it was a consolation, that if they were occasionally a little way behind, there was barely a possibility of their being thrown out. A pack of this description was perfectly accommodating to the neighbouring rustics, the major part of those not being possessed of horses found it a matter of no great difficulty to be well up with them on foot. The spirit of emulation seemed formerly to be who should produce the greatest degree of merit in the smallest compass; and packs were to be seen in different parts of the most diminutive description.
>
> Among professed amateurs every effort was made to attain perfection, and these indefatigable endeavours were generally attended with success. Beagles were almost uniformly so well matched, that they did not exceed ten or eleven inches in height, and so carefully selected in respect to speed, that whenever they were running they might be covered with a sheet; and this alone is the predominant trait of celebrity in a pack of hounds, or beagles,

whether great or small. These, though slow, are incredibly destructive; for if the scent lays well, the hare has very little chance of escape, and this to the object of pursuit must prove a lingering, as well as a certain death; for although in the early parts of the chase they can never get near enough the hare to press her, yet they are in general finally fatal, if even three or four hours in killing. In proportion to the increasing spirit of sporting and polish of the times, slow hunting declined, and beagles became of less repute; it being now exceedingly uncommon to see any collection of beagles beyond two or three couple, used in some districts where hares, from a variety of circumstances, are known to be scarce or with difficulty to be found.

From this it is clear that at the beginning of the nineteenth century the beagle was in a sharp decline. It was out of fashion. The old simplicity of the countryside was beginning to falter in the face of the new fashions of speed and manners. But it will be worth while to follow the *Sportsman's Cabinet* a little farther, for the author has much of interest to say on the beagle itself.

The numerous and diversified crosses in the different breeds of both beagles and hounds, according to the views, wishes, and inclinations of those who keep them, have so complicated and variegated that particular part of the species, that a volume might be produced in describing the various sorts and sizes, as thought best adapted to the soil and surface for which they are bred and intended to hunt; from the old, heavy, deep-tongued, dew-lapped, southern hound of Lancashire (where the huntsman with his pole follows on foot) to the fleetest bred northern harriers of the present day, who kill their game in a burst of half an hour or forty minutes with a degree of rapidity little inferior to coursing.

The breed of hounds now passing under the denomination of harriers, have been brought to their present state of perfection, by a repetition of crosses between the beagle and the foxhound, for the increase in size and promotion of speed; but beagles, in the sporting acceptation of the term, are not to be considered synonymous with harriers, to whom, although they possess precisely the same properties, they are very much inferior in size. That some adequate idea may be formed of the original beagle, the following ludicrous transaction is introduced from the most indisputable authority:

The late Col. Hardy had once a collection of this diminutive tribe amounting to ten or twelve couple, which were always carried to and from the field of glory in a large pair of panniers slung across a horse; small as they were, and insignificant as they would now seem, they could invariably keep a hare at all her shifts to escape them, and finally worry, or rather teaze her to death. The catastrophe attending which curious pack was of a very singular description; for a small barn having some time appropriated to the purpose of a kennel, was one night broke open, and every hound as well as the panniers stolen; nor could the most diligent search ever discover the least trace of the robbers, or their sporting appendage.

Perhaps that, written in the doldrums of beagling, shows as clearly as anything is ever likely to do the origin of the little hound. And it is clear from this writer that in its earlier hey-day the art of beagling reached in some ways a higher pitch than it has ever reached since. To describe a pack in full cry as so well knit that it could be covered with a sheet is praise indeed, and even allowing something for poetic licence and the enthusiasm of a disciple, it indicates a perfection that few packs of the present day could approach.

During the doldrums the beagle was little used for hare-hunting. It is made quite clear by Johnson in the *Sportsman's Cyclopædia*, which was published in 1830, that then the beagle, which had apparently sunk yet farther, was not used for more than a mere adjunct to coursing. He says: " They were originally employed for the purpose of coursing: they would trail a hare to her form, or, by opening, give notice that one was at no great distance." They were then, in fact, not hare-hunters but hare-finders.

The doldrums fortunately did not last for a very long time. About the fifties of the last century the beagle began to come back into popular favour. By the sixties there was a miniature boom. The Royal Rock, the oldest pack still in existence, was founded in 1845. By the sixties there were several with a good member-ship, and from then on the beagle has steadily advanced in popularity.

The modern beagle is a truly splendid little hound, bred for stamina and hunting qualities, and of quite astonishing speed. Running with a pack of beagles can be very hard exercise indeed, and requires from the followers a fund of stamina of the very first order. In fact, there are packs of 15-inch beagles which on a good scent will leave all foot followers behind and would tax a horse for a short space of time. It has always astonished me that with this excellent sport to be had for the asking, and with inter-national competition in long-distance and cross-country running at the pitch at which it now stands, our long-distance runners are not trained over the country behind the beagles. I am sure the result in International matches would be most gratifying if this practice was adopted, and that Great Britain would do much better at the next Olympic Marathon.

In essentials the modern beagle, so far as points are concerned, differs little from the foxhound. At present, in order to come within the Stud Book limit, the beagle must be under 16 inches in height. He should have really good sloping shoulders without any " lumpiness " and a reasonably long neck. In a bitch the neck should be really long and fine. The dog's neck should naturally be heavier, but in both dogs and bitches there should be no fullness or coarseness. The forelegs should be absolutely straight, ending in cat paws, with the toes held well together, and the bone of the leg carried down into the foot so that there is absolutely no appearance of an ankle. The bone of the foreleg from the elbow to the foot must be large, really large; a beagle should have forelegs that look much thicker than would seem necessary. The ribs must be well sprung and really deep. The chest should extend an inch or so below the point of the elbow. This with well-sprung ribs will give the necessary room for the lungs and the heart. It should never be forgotten that the most necessary qualification in a beagle is heart room. The ribs should be carried well back, so that the animal is well coupled, and the back should be flat and short, the loins powerful, the quarters muscular, and the hocks very close to the ground. The stern, which should be thick at the base, should come off the level spine at right angles. Normally it should be carried straight and perpendicular, but a slight curve over the back is not objected to.

A good hound always seems to have a good head. A good beagle head should be set on the neck at an easy angle, should be larger in the dog than in the bitch, but should not be too large in the one or too small in the other. The eye should be kindly and set wide, and the very large ear should be hung low on the head. The true hound look is given, of course, by deep flews and a good length of muzzle, but the appearance of a beagle is not that of a foxhound. A beagle has a cheery look about him. I have never yet seen a foxhound that looked as if it had a sense of humour (though I have known one or two that most definitely had one), but I have never yet seen a good beagle that did not at first sight seem to have a real sense of fun.

The colour of a beagle, so long as it is a hound colour, does not matter. Chocolate, in the Show Ring, is not admired, but beyond this it seems to be the fact that every hound colour has its admirers. Whatever the colour, the stern must be tipped with white.

There is a good deal of difference of opinion as to the right height for a pack of beagles. The limit imposed at the Hound Show at Peterborough is 16 inches at the shoulder. This is the Stud Book limit. But there are several packs hunting in England whose hounds are over 16 inches in height. Actually, no matter what the limit imposed by the Stud Book, the best size for a pack of beagles is determined by the nature of the country to be hunted. If the country is open and hilly, or if it contains miles of heather or bracken, it is obvious that the hounds have got to be big and strong, at least 16 inches, and probably more. But if the country is not too large and there is plenty of plough and grass alternating, then a pack of 14½ hounds will be big enough. The trouble with hounds of 16 inches and over is that they are so fast that the majority of the field cannot keep anywhere near them under any conditions, and when in pursuit of a straight-running hare they will leave any man living well behind.

So far as England is concerned, the Basset is quite a recent breed. The first basset hound ever shown in England was one named " Model ", which was imported from France by Sir Everett Millais in 1874 and exhibited at Wolverhampton in 1875. Bassets had been known in Ireland before this, but had not been used for hunting. Millais crossed his " Model " with a beagle, and in 1876 showed the cross at Wolverhampton, but the breed did not catch on until 1881, when a number of hounds were imported from France and the Basset Hound Club was formed. By 1890 the breed had become popular and was well established, and now it may truly be said that there has been evolved an English basset.

The basset, as has been shown, is really a French breed. It does not seem to be a very old breed even in France, and no one appears to know how or when it originated. At one time there were several different sorts of bassets, each following more or less closely the various breeds of full-sized hounds, but these gradually died out, and there can be little doubt that the breed from which all present types spring came originally from Artois and Flanders. Though there is only one type in England (that is, only one breed known as the basset hound), there are still four distinct breeds of bassets to be found in France.   These are the Artois and Vendeen breeds, which are by far the most common, and the Blue Gascon and Fawn Breton breeds, which are now becoming distinctly uncommon.

The English basset hound normally stands between 14 and 15 inches in height, though there is one pack in the country with hounds between 16 and 18 inches in height.   This is the Brancaster, and the reason for the greater height is that this pack, alone of English packs, is hunted on horseback.   The old idea, which was the idea of the Basset Hound Club (now defunct) which was formed for the show bench only, of hounds with crooked forelegs and ears long enough to be trodden on, has quite gone.   No one could hunt hare with hounds weighing 40 lb. and standing on 4-inch forelegs, and crooked forelegs at that.   Legs are now straight and strong, with great bone and substance.   The basset is now truly a hound for hunting the hare.

Chapter III

HUNTING THE HARE

Over the edge of the rabbit-trimmed down
There you go crippling, crippling.
Lonely and wind-blown and ruddily brown,
Wearing in Northlands a white winter gown,
There you go crippling, crippling.

A. J. H.

SO you may hunt the hare with harriers, with beagles or with bassets. Let me say at once that I know very little from personal experience of hunting with harriers, and but little more of hunting with bassets. My opportunities have come in the main with beagles.

Hunting with harriers is horseman's business, and I have always thought that hare-hunting ought to be done on foot. Hunting harriers, therefore, is in many ways fox-hunting in miniature. There is not so much difference in the management of harriers and foxhounds, though it should always be remembered that the harrier is of a more gentle temperament. Both harriers and foxhounds require firm handling, of course, to prevent the formation of bad habits, but the harrier needs much quieter handling. I have seen a hound put off hunting for the whole day because the Whip was much too severe, and I have heard that it is possible to ruin a hound altogether by being too severe. There can be no doubt, too, that the business of hunting harriers requires greater patience than does

40

hunting foxhounds. Especially is this so on a bad scenting day. On such a day the hare has plenty of time to play tricks (of which all hares have a good repertoire), and this means that one has always to be pulling up one's horse. Furthermore, on such a day hounds are apt suddenly to run very fast, and invariably when they do they overrun the line. Not infrequently when this happens the Field have followed up quickly, too, thinking that at last they are going to get away on a straight-running hare, and then the ground is foiled, and a good deal of time may be lost in casting around to hit off the line. What has happened, of course, is that the hare, knowing a good deal more about scenting conditions than the hounds or the huntsman, and knowing that she has plenty of time, has run up and down the same line several times, and so left a strong scent, before taking a great jump sideways and going off at right angles. That sort of thing is pretty common in hare-hunting with harriers. It is, in fact, a common jibe among fox-hunters that hares always run in a circle, and that if you know anything about hunting you need never bother to do more than jog along around the centre, and the hunt will sooner or later come back to you. It is not true; though there is a good deal of truth in it. It is not true, for example, if you happen to come across a travelling jack. But it is true that for the most part hares know their country and stick to it. It is only when a hare has been bustled off her country that she will run fast and straight, and then the hare-hunt may well resemble a fox-hunt with a fast, straight run of several miles. Such occasions are not frequent in a season. But though I have called hunting harriers fox-hunting in miniature, there is one great difference. The majority of people who hunt the fox do so for the thrill of a good gallop over good country with plenty of jumps. Indeed, I have sometimes wondered whether hounds were really necessary. Very few people who hunt the fox can watch hound-work, and fewer still want to do so. The gallop and the jumps are the attractions. They most certainly are not the attractions of harriers. The thrills of good fast galloping and plenty of jumping over good country are few and far between. But the opportunities of watching hound-work are many. And whereas the foxhound needs a good deal of help from the huntsman, harriers really need very little. They are much more likely to pick out a line if left to themselves. There is therefore the added pleasure of watching good hound-work by hounds themselves without aid (or interference!) from the huntsman.

Hare-hunting with harriers is not so popular as once it was and, with the exception of the West country, there are to-day fewer packs of harriers. I think this is a pity, for though I do not myself think that hunting the hare with harriers can compare as a sport with beagling, I do think that harriers and foxhounds should go hand in hand, and that a pack of harriers, properly managed, is an advantage to a fox-hunting country. Perhaps the economic conditions that are going to prevail for many years to come will mean some revival in harriers in those districts in which hitherto the fox has reigned supreme.

Basset hound-packs, too, are few and far between. And this is indeed a pity. For I believe that the basset is the ideal type of hound for hare-hunting. Harriers are too prone to race a hare down without giving it a sporting chance, and they are by no means sure on a catchy scent. Beagles are, of course, wonderful little hounds, game and full of life, but though I give place to no man in my admiration for them, it cannot be denied that they are not sure on a very light scent. But the basset has a wonderful nose on the lightest of scents, and is extraordinarily determined. They are, moreover, not fast—nothing like fast enough to run down a fresh hare—and this means that the hares they catch are caught as the result of a fair hunt and good hound-work. And there is one further point about the basset. He has the most beautiful music of any hound.

But we have—and may all the Saints be praised—beagles, and plenty of them. And though I have a lingering fondness for the basset and an idea that that hound is the ideal type for the sport of hare-hunting (though I have had but few opportunities of following basset hounds), my heart is really given to the beagle. There was a time when I asked for no better day than a day spent in the company of beagles. Increasing age and increasing girth take me more frequently to the river's edge nowadays, for I find the sport of Angling—a contemplative sport—more suited to the present stage of my sojourn on this earth, but still the music of beagles stirs my blood, and even stirs my legs to unwonted (if short-lived) activity.

Beagling is a very great sport. It is a very great sport in itself, but so is fox-hunting. Beagling has become a greater sport because it has remained free from all outside influences. It has never become fashionable; it has never become expensive: it has remained free from all traces of snobbery. It has remained, above all things, a sport. No man and no woman has ever used, I am sure, beagling as a rung of the social ladder. The same cannot be said of the fox-hunting of the inter-war period. So far as I am aware, no prosperous City merchant has ever driven down to the country of a Saturday morning and run with the beagles for the rest of the day, unless he has been really keen on beagling. The same cannot be said of fashionable fox-hunting. Fox-hunting may be democratic (but if you read John Moore's *Portrait of Elmbury* you may be persuaded that it is also something else), but no one who is not entirely biased can pretend that there is not in the fashionable hunts more than a modicum of snobbery. The fact is that you can hunt the fox without being in the least interested in fox-hunting as such, and it is also a fact that you cannot hunt the fox with the majority of the packs in this country unless you have money—or a great deal of credit. But you can follow the beagles anywhere in the British Isles, and no one will care a hoot if you are wealthy or if you are " broke ". And you cannot follow the beagles unless you are interested—and very interested at that—in hunting the hare. What it comes down to is this: there are no horses attached to beagling. You have got to run on your own feet. You are down to earth. You are mounted not on what money will buy, but on what God gave you. And that is true of the whole field. The whole sport is down to earth. And thank God for it.

The beagler must be a hound-lover before all else. I do not believe that most beaglers regard the sport primarily as a blood sport—in fact, I am sure that no true beagler ever does so. The men and women who follow the beagles do so because it provides exercise in a form that cannot be equalled in any other way, and because it provides opportunities for watching hounds at work that no other sport can provide—if the music of hounds does not mean anything to you, you will not become a beagler; I am sure that much of the fascination of the sport lies in the magic of the music of hounds—and beside these things the kill is a matter of small importance. The kill is, of course, a fitting ending to a good hunt. It is no more than that. The fact that some packs kill almost every time they go out does not mean that they are good packs, certainly does not mean that they are better packs than those that kill less frequently. I confess to regarding with some suspicion packs that finish the season with a very large number of hares accounted for in proportion to the number of times they have been out.   It generally means that the hounds are too big for their their country, that the hares are over-matched in point of speed and endurance, and that they are raced to death without a hunt. There is no hound-work about that sort of thing.

This brings up the question of size again.   As I have already said, this is governed to a great extent by the sort of country that is to be hunted.   You could not hunt 14½-inch beagles over a mountain country, or over a country with much heather, or over a country of big stone walls.   They would be tired out before the day was very old.   For such countries beagles of 16 inches, or even more, are essential, and the hare is neither over-matched in speed nor in endurance.   But a pack that size on average English country, where plough and grass alternate, will either chop the hare before the animal has a chance, which is not beagling, or leave the field so far behind so quickly that they see nothing at all, which also is not beagling.   It should always be remembered that not all of the Field are young, and that not all of the young members are fast.   And it should always be remembered that all the Field, whether they be young or old, fast or slow, are out because they are beaglers and want to see hounds at work.   All this can be done if hounds match their country.   Unfortunately this is not yet the case all over England.

Most people should be able to keep up with a 14½-inch pack. Of course, something depends on the fitness of the man or woman concerned.   There was a time when I ran with the beagles regularly, and I was then living a country life, taking a good deal of exercise in the normal course of the day, and keeping, without doing any training, as fit as maybe.   Then I did not have much difficulty in keeping up with hounds all day.   There was also a time when I was able to run with the beagles on only one afternoon a week, or more often one afternoon a fortnight.   My standard of fitness then was very different.   Keeping anywhere near them became a matter of very considerable difficulty.   But I generally managed to see most of the run, and I think that I was always within hearing of the music.   And that, so far as I was concerned—and I think that it would satisfy most beaglers—was all that mattered.   It is largely a matter of common sense, this keeping within sight.   The exercise of common sense will balance a good deal of unfitness.   But no amount of common sense will balance a pack that is too big for its country.

So, taking an average country—plough and grass, hedges and not walls—I believe the smaller the size of beagles the better. The smaller the hounds, the closer they hunt the line of the hare, the slower they run, the better the music they give. And what more can one want of beagles than that? But I do not believe that beagles should go below 14 inches.

Just as important as size is level. A wonderfully level pack that I had the great pleasure of running with once or twice was the Airedale. I have run with one or two others that are probably just as level, but the Airedale stick in my mind because of the excellent sport they showed each time I was out with them. A really good beagle pack should run as a pack. There should not be a leader out in front and one or two hounds tailing along in the rear. Too frequently this is just what does happen. I can understand why the leaders in such cases are not drafted; they are good hounds, perhaps outstanding hounds, and there is a natural pride in their possession and in their abilities. But I can never understand why the tailers are not drafted. I have known more than one pack which would have been improved a great deal had the tailers been discarded. I have known still more packs that would have been vastly improved had leading hounds been drafted. Such hounds do more harm than is generally realised, for in time they affect every hound behind them, since these hounds come to run on the sight of the leader and not on the scent. It is very much better to have a level pack than a pack containing one or two brilliant performers. It should be the aim of every Master of beagles to have a pack like that immortalised in *The Sportsman's Cabinet*, a pack so well knit that when running it could be covered by a sheet. To that ideal outstanding hounds should be sacrificed, to that ideal should be sacrificed brilliance and speed. Level should be the target, the supreme aim.

The question of level brings up the much greater question of hound-breeding. This is a subject I am not in the least qualified to write about, and for that reason I do not intend to do so. But one or two observations on the subject generally may perhaps be forgiven me.

Animal-breeding—no matter what sort of animal, whether thoroughbreds or cattle or hounds—is a science. Too often in books about hunting you will find hound-breeding referred to as a " fascinating pursuit ". Of course it is—so is growing dahlias—but it is also a science. And this is rather too often forgotten. A perfunctory reading of some book on genetics, a nodding acquaintance with the Mendelian law of segregation, and all seems to be set for embarking upon " the fascinating pursuit ". And then you will find some breeder complaining that though much valuable work has been done by the scientists, they are out of touch with practical breeders and their problems. The fact is, of course, that the practical breeder is not so practical as all that, and is a little out of touch with the scientists.

Pedigree by itself is not enough. Pedigree is of great importance, but in two animals of equally good pedigree, performance is the deciding factor—or should be. Looks are certainly not so important as performance. In dog-breeding generally breeders have concentrated on some particular point of conformation—in other words, on looks—and the result is plain to see. In many cases it has proved disastrous to the quality of the breed. No one could pretend that the collie is as good a working dog as it used to be; the bull-terrier has lost all the qualities that made the breed famous; most of the terrier breeds have been ruined in order to succeed on the Show Bench. Nothing like that has happened to the hound. Foxhounds, harriers, beagles are still bred for use. Yet, with one or two shining examples as exceptions, there was creeping in before the war a tendency to put too much stress on conformation, and that could be done only at the expense of performance.

So far as beagles are concerned, it is very much easier to breed a good large hound than a good small one. Why that should be so I do not know, but that it is so a visit to any beagle kennels will prove conclusively. Perhaps it has something to do with the great reliance that is placed upon the dog in breeding. In book after book you will find the stress laid on the qualities of the dog. All the books will tell you to use the best bitches you have available, but all the books will tell you to get the best stallion hound you can, even if it means searching the country. I cannot believe that the bitch is as unimportant comparatively as that. The beagle is being bred below its natural size. Of that there can be no doubt. The natural size of a beagle is between 16 and 18 inches. There is absolutely no reason why the size should not become fixed in just the same way as one can fix other qualities in an animal. But, to fix size, as great attention must be paid to the female as to the male, and over many generations. This does not apply so forcibly to foxhounds (there are some wonderful and very good-looking packs of foxhounds), since the foxhound is bred to his natural size. It is even possible to breed level packs of crossed English and Welsh foxhound blood: Lady Curre's is an outstanding example of this.

There has always been much discussion whether constant out-crossing or close in-breeding is the most likely to produce a good pack of hounds. To produce a level pack of foxhounds it seems that the modified form of in-breeding known as line-breeding is the most suitable. Myself, I am very doubtful if that is the case with beagles. The scientists maintain that the only way to im-prove stock is to inbreed closely to the best animals and to practise rigorous selection. This system made our live stock what it is. The system tends to make the resulting strain extremely prepotent when used for breeding, and it tends to make individuals resemble each other closely. From the size point of view this is just what is wanted in beagles. And though it is true that by close in-breeding you fix bad qualities in a strain as well as good ones, this can be overcome by rigorous selection.

There is, however, another point. Animal-breeding is a long-term business. The British thoroughbred was not produced in a year, nor yet in twenty. The Dairy Shorthorn was not evolved overnight. To which kennels do you go for your foxhound blood? Successful hound-breeding is no less a long-term business. But nowadays Masters do not stay for many years in their Master-ships. Before the war they were continually changing. There seems to be little prospect of this process altering in the near future.

The Master of foxhounds has more to contend with than just the fox and his hounds and his horse. He has also the Field. Fox-hunting Fields sometimes become a little unruly, and Masters of foxhounds have, largely as a result of this, acquired a reputa-tion for a command of colourful language, a reputation that is not wholly undeserved. Masters of beagles are more fortunate. Beagling Fields are rarely unruly. On the contrary, they are usually remarkably well-behaved. And in beagling, no less than in fox-hunting, a well-behaved Field is an essential to a good day's sport.

In beagling the Field is under the direct control of the Field

Master. It is his duty to keep them in the correct position. Whilst drawing in the open, hounds are kept reasonably close to the Master. The Field is organised by the Field Master, and spread out in a line so that they do not interfere with the hounds, or get in the way of any of the officials. They are therefore spread out in a line behind the hounds, so that no matter how close hares may squat, should the hounds overlook one, she will be put up by the followers. It may seem unlikely that a hare would squat while hounds and officials and, say, a Field of more than a hundred people walk over the field, and perhaps almost over her, but it has happened many times, and will happen again. The Field is therefore spread out in a line about 60 yards behind hounds—they should never be nearer than 50 yards—and the Master will cast his hounds backwards and forwards parallel to this line. By this means any hare that is put up will be reasonably close to hounds and should have to exert herself to avoid the first rush.

As a rule the first check is met with soon after the start; the first time, in fact, that the hare is out of sight. The hare will use this opportunity in any of a dozen ways, but she will almost certainly not go straight on. In their excitement—particularly if this is the first hare of the day—hounds will probably over-run the scent. Now, the behaviour of the Field is important. They can either ruin the hunt, or they can give the hounds a chance to recover the line. A good Field will have kept a little way behind hounds, and so soon as they see that they have lost the scent they will keep quite still and quite quiet. A talking Field is a menace of the first class. Hounds at their first check should, in my opinion, be allowed to cast back of their own accord. I have noticed that if they are so allowed they will hunt the better for the rest of the day. But it is not only the Field that can interfere at this initial check. The humble rabbit can also do so, and often does. I have not yet met a pack of beagles that will not be led astray by a rabbit. They are all right while in active pursuit of a hare, but at checks it is quite a different matter. I do not think that it is fair to blame the beagles for this; there is not so much difference between a hare and a rabbit as all that. But I once saw a pack at a check go off in full cry after a French partridge. It is one of the few occasions on which I have seen a Frenchman take wing without hesitation!

A fresh hare, after the initial check, causes little trouble while she remains fresh. It is when she becomes tired, when the hunt is beginning to tell upon her, that she starts to use her brains. Then one sees the full cunning of a really clever animal. One of her favourite dodges is to run through a hedge so as to be out of sight and to run on into the field for about fifty yards: she will double back exactly on her line and then run back into the hedge, along which she will turn, and, by means of great jumps (and she is capable of jumping astonishing distances), move away to one side or the other, leaving as little scent as possible. If the Field has come through the hedge, it is more likely than not that hounds will never pick up the line again, and that the hare will be clear away.

Another favourite trick is for the hare to run through a hedge or to put some other obstacle between her and the hunt so as to be out of sight, and then, when in the middle of a field, to run round and round in circles before taking a great leap off to one side or the other. This is very puzzling for hounds, and needs careful handling by the Master. I have more than once seen a hare get clean away by means of this trick. And I once saw a hare that had obviously done this add a refinement to it, and get clear away as a result. After taking her great leaps to one side, she had sat close—in the same big field as the hounds—and then, suddenly jumping up, she came rushing through the Field and back to the hedge. What she did then I do not know, but hounds were unable to pick up her line again.

Hares will put up a fresh hare when they are getting tired, squatting where the fresh hare squatted. This is, of course, a favourite trick, and I have sometimes wondered whether there is not some collusion between hares in the matter. It would be foolish to say that hares enjoy being hunted—nothing makes me more angry than to be told by an ardent fox-hunter that one of the chief reasons for fox-hunting is that the fox enjoys it—for I am quite sure that the hare no more enjoys being hunted than we should like being hunted. But whereas I have never seen a fox who looked as if he enjoyed the idea of foxhounds on his trail, I have more than once seen a hare that appeared to be playing with hounds. And I imagine that every beagler has had the same experience. I believe that every hare thinks at the commencement of a hunt that she is going to get away pretty easily. I am quite sure that no hare, upon being put up by beagles, immediately thinks that her last day has come and runs merely from panic. And she has grounds for belief in her own powers. A large proportion of

D

hares do get away, not only the first time, but many times. Indeed, the only reason why hares are caught, supposing that they are not overmatched, is because they are animals of comparatively small stamina, whereas the beagle is an animal of very considerable stamina. So at the start the hare, fresh, is full of confidence, and the tiring hare that puts up a fresh hare (and presumably the latter is willing to be put up) is putting up an animal full of confidence.

But the wiles of the hare do not end there. They will use, and are adepts at using, anything that does not hold scent. They will run down roads or along railway lines; they will use ditches and swim rivers. I have known one run along the top of a wall for quite a considerable distance. And the hare knows a lot more about the scenting conditions than the Master does or, for that matter, than the hounds do. Scent is, despite the learned tomes that have been written about it, a mystery to man. We do not know why scent should be good on some days and poor on others. We have all sorts of ideas, and some of them no doubt come fairly near the truth, but we do not know. The hare, I think, does know. At least, the behaviour of a hare on a day of " catchy " scent is from the very first different from that of a hare on a day of good holding scent. And it must be remembered that beagles are only one of many enemies of the hare, and certainly not the most important, and the hare is using not only her cunning and her knowledge of local conditions, but also her knowledge of scent, all the time in the preservation of her life.

To return to the Field. Before the war Fields were increasing in size, due in the main to the motor-car. In the days of my youth a good Field with my local beagles was twenty-five. Not long before the war I saw a Field of some two hundred with these same beagles. From the point of view of the Hunt Finances this was all to the good. But it is not an unmixed blessing, and some Masters, I have heard tell, dislike big Fields very much. They will have to get used to them. For I am convinced that there is going to be a big boom in beagling before long, and these big Fields will come to stay, for once a beagler always a beagler. They will need some education to begin with, and the most essential education will be to teach them that they see more of the hunt from a little distance than when on the top of the hounds. They will also have to be taught that one can have too much " viewing ". I am, personally, and speaking as one who brings up the rear, all against members of the Field holloaing at all, and I believe that most Masters would agree with that opinion. Fields should be trained by the Field Master to indicate a view by waving a cap or a scarf or handkerchief.

And what should the beagler wear? Hunt uniform in the beagling world is worn at the invitation of the Master. Coats, stockings and caps are usually green, and breeches white. It is indeed a proud moment when one is asked to wear the uniform of the Hunt. But that is an honour that comes to comparatively few of the Field. What should the ordinary beagler wear? There was once a standard about these things, but standards were beginning to die before the war, and now coupons will have killed them. They are even beginning to disappear from the City—that fortress of conventional attire. I think that the only standard that will be accepted for a long while to come will be that of suitability. What is suitable for beagling? Well, I have run after the beagles in shorts and a sweater, and personally I regard that dress as eminently suitable to the occasion. There are Masters who would not agree with me. But really there is no reason why any but the hunt officials should dress the part. Suitability does not mean formality, but it does mean comfort. Clothes, therefore, should be light. That is most important. And it is a good idea, especially if you are getting past the first flush of youth, to have clothes that are both windproof and waterproof. You might think that running after the beagles is a warm enough business in itself, and that there is no reason why one should worry about clothes being windproof. But the whole day is not spent running after beagles. Quite a lot of it is spent in standing around. The top of a hill in January and a cold north wind is not the most comfortable of places, and windproof clothing is then a boon indeed. I have seen a man become so cold at such a wait that he has not been able to run when hounds moved off again. Dress is important so far as comfort is concerned, but shoes are very important indeed. They must be light, and they must be able to stand a good deal of knocking about. It is my opinion that the ordinary walking-shoe is quite useless, no matter who the maker. The ordinary boot is a good deal worse. For several seasons I did run in boots, but they were hockey boots, canvas-sided, and as light as a feather. They wore well, too, for they had done a good deal of service on the hockey-field before they were entered to the beagles. I do not believe it would be possible to improve upon them for beagling, and they are a definite advance on shoes, for they do provide some support for the ankle. When at last they gave out I took to canvas tennis shoes with crepe soles. These were light enough, and they had the advantage (which does not hold good nowadays!) that they were cheap and could easily be replaced when they wore out, which was pretty soon. They had, however, one great disadvantage, in that the soles were so thin that they let you know about every stone or sharp edge throughout the day. I do not know if hockey boots are still made, but if they are, I know well what my choice would be were I to beagle again.

I have left to the last one of the most important factors in a well-run pack of beagles—the whippers-in. As a follower, and a follower well in the rear, I have had plenty of opportunity of watching whips, and I hold strong views on whips. To begin with, I think that most packs are under-staffed in this department. I do not know how many whips are considered necessary to a well-run hunt, but the number seems to be two as a general rule. And as a general rule two is not enough. I would far rather see a hunt over-whipped than one under-staffed. Is there any reason why there should not be, say, six whips in the field? The number of occasions in this country nowadays when hounds have to be stopped from going into some place or other—and there will be more of these occasions in the future—is enormous, and the more whips you have the less trouble you have. Again, whips are human (some Masters seem to doubt this), and they tire if they have too much to do. I know that it is hard enough to find an efficient whip anyhow, and it may well be that Masters have given up trying to find more than two that are efficient. After all, the qualities in a really good whip are not easy to find. He must be, first and foremost, a really good long-distance runner and a really strong man, for heavy plough all day will take it out of the strongest. He must have really good sight. He must use that sight in an intelligent manner; in other words, he must be observant. He must be really keen on hunting. He must know all the hounds by name. He must be tactful. He must be very unselfish, for as a whip he may have but little sport throughout the day. He must be good-tempered. And he must have a pronounced sense of humour. In how many men will you find all those qualities? In very few. Yet I have met quite a number of perfect whips.

And I have seen some really good whips ruined by overwork. It would be better from the point of view of the hunt, of the sport, and of the whips (which in the long run means also of the Master), if there were more whips per hunt. Obviously they would not all be as efficient as the Master would wish—but, then, I have an idea that no whip is ever as efficient as the Master would wish—but they would, if picked carefully, soon make for greater efficiency in the field and greater enjoyment for the followers, and that should be the object of every Master.

And what happens when the hare has been killed? By the way, beagles do not hunt, I am sure, just because they want to kill hares. All my experience tends to show that they are much more interested in scent than in the hare herself, and they take little notice of her once they have killed. There is very little worrying of the corpse. All the same, trophies may be ruined if the corpse is not taken as soon as possible. Many a good mask has been ruined, too, by being cut off too short. Sufficient skin must be left to allow it to be mounted to the best advantage. The skin should be cut at the shoulder-blades, and just in front of the forelegs. Closer to the skull than that and the taxidermist will not be able to make a job of it. After the pads and the mask have been removed, the rest of the hare is the business of the hounds.

Chapter IV

MORE WAYS THAN ONE

Halloo-Halloo-See, see from yonder Furze
The Lurchers have alarm'd and started Puss!
Hold! What d'ye do? Sure you don't mean to Fire!
Constrain that base, ungenerous Desire,
And let the Courser and the Huntsman share
Their just and proper Title to the Hare.
Let the poor Creature pass, and have fair play,
And fight the Prize of Life out her own Way.
The tracing Hound by Nature was design'd
Both for the Use and Pleasure of Mankind;
Form'd for the Hare, the Hare too for the Hound:
In enmity each to each other bound:
Then he who dares by different means destroy
Than Nature meant, offends 'gainst NATURE's Law.

George Markland.

THERE are other legitimate means of catching hares than by hunting. You may course them with hounds, or you may shoot them. We have already seen what William Somervile thought of coursing. We do not know what he thought of shooting hares, but it would not be difficult to guess. The above quotation is from *Pteryplegia, or, The Art of Shooting Flying*. It shows quite clearly what Markland thought of shooting hares. But it also shows that he did not disapprove, as did Somervile, of coursing. And there you have it. You may approve of hunting the hare with hounds and disapprove of coursing and shooting. You may approve of coursing and dislike shooting. You may approve of shooting and disapprove of the other sports. There are some people who approve of them all. There are even, I believe, people who disapprove of them all; though what they think would happen to the hare population if all three should be stopped I cannot guess.

My own view is that of Somervile. I do not like coursing. I do not regard it as a sport. It was once. But private coursing, of the type beloved by Charles Richardson, is dead in this country, though fortunately that is not the case in Ireland, where they still breed the best greyhounds. There was great sport in the old private coursing meet, as all those who are familiar with Richardson's writings will know. At those meets the hare was not overmatched in any way (indeed, she as frequently as not beat the hounds; Richardson records thirty courses in succession at one meet without a hare being killed), and there was a real test of the ability and speed of the hounds. Furthermore, at the old private meet there was no bias in favour of money. Any one could turn up, and any one could enter a hound if he had one he thought good enough. Richardson's records of the North-country meets are revealing in this respect. Well, all that has gone. I do not object to coursing because I think it is cruel. I do not think that it is any more cruel than many other things that go on in this country, and not nearly as cruel as some. I do not like coursing simply because I do not think that it is any longer a sport. The hare is overmatched. Not by the hounds alone—that certainly is not the case—but by the adornments to modern coursing meets: the stops, the beaters, the crowds, the confined space—things that were absent from the old private meet. And with all this the free-and-easy democracy of coursing has disappeared altogether from this country. If you think that that is an exaggerated statement, go over to Ireland and watch coursing there. Coursing, it seems to me, has in England ceased to be a sport, and become a rich man's amusement. And it has developed other and less pleasing features—amongst other things, heavy betting. I do not know that greyhound-track racing is any better test of the respective merits of the hounds—I should be inclined to doubt it—but at least it does not call itself a sport, and as an amusement it is very much better organised.

Before we come to shooting, there is the most ancient and, I imagine, the grandest of sports to be considered—namely, hawking. I have done but little hawking, and my knowledge of the sport is just about nil. But I know I would rather potter round the hedgerows with a hawk on my fist than with a twelve-bore under my arm.

And in this I am in good company, for you will remember Patrick
Chalmers, now, alas! no longer here to delight us with his delicate
fancy: " Yet I have sometimes thought if, instead of a gun, I might
carry a goshawk, a handy lady goshawk (*Diamond*, I shall call her),
riding unhooded and in eager *yarak* upon my fist, that a spice of
novelty and romance would be lent to the golden November noon
when to mouch is most indicated." Patrick was of the opinion
that a goshawk would be just as good a companion for the potterer
as a gun, and a much more amusing one. And I agree. I agree,
too, that the goshawk is the only true substitute for the gun. There
are other hawks, of course, and there are falcons. But they have
as much relation to the goshawk as driven grouse have to the sport
of ordinary mortals. Let me quote again: " The falcons,
peregrine, and ger, who, stooping from the high and exalted blue,
will, for the delight of their masters, knock down an old and
desperately dodging October grouse, knock him down, dead as
any door-nail, on his own dark heath; the falcons, sirs, could they
be substitutes for anything but thunder-bolts? " And the merlin,
too, " the friendly little practice hawk of the 'prentice, is a miniature
falcon and mounts as such; also she is too light to hold a rabbit or
a hare, even would she be wishful to ' fly ' one ". No; it must be
the goshawk or nothing for the man who wants a substitute for the
gun. And I have never owned a goshawk. And only once have
I flown one.

Continually there are attempts to revive the sport of falconry
in this country. There is a Falconers' Club, and there can be no
doubt that there is a good deal of interest in the sport. I am
frequently asked by boys at public schools to find them a trained
hawk or falcon, and sometimes I succeed. But the sport will not
come back to popular favour, I fear, for the simple reason that it
is a simple sport. It was the sport of Kings and Princes. It was
the sport of all men who wanted it in the grand Elizabethan days,
when all men were princes in some sort, when the simple was not
disdained, when the record had not become the god of all sport.
Too frequently nowadays sport is judged not by its quality, but
solely by the quantity of game killed. Record bags, record days,
record rents. Well, you cannot get a record bag with a hawk or
a falcon. Your record day will compare unfavourably with the
record day of the man with the twelve-bore. No one will pay you
a record rent for the privilege of flying his hawk over your ground.

"The goshawk is the only true substitute for the gun." Goshawk and leveret.

It remains a simple sport, and, unfortunately, there are few simple men in the world to-day.

Yet in some sense it may be considered, along with hunting the hare, our national sport. Which sports do we find mentioned most often in the works of the greatest of our poets? William Shakespeare speaks more frequently of hunting and falconry, and that he knew both sports from personal experience is beyond doubt. But, then, Shakespeare was a country lad—and there are those who maintain that he came to London only because he was a poacher who had been caught (if so, there is more to be said for poaching than the landlord would have us believe)—and a country lad at a time when sport was sport throughout the land. Yes, Shakespeare knew falconry from personal experience. Of that there can be no doubt. Many a time he must have flown his own birds. You will remember that he makes Warwick say:

> Neither the king, nor he that loves him best,
> The proudest he that holds up Lancaster,
> Dares stir a wing, if Warwick shake his bells.

And if you have ever seen a covey of partridges clap down where a falcon " waits on " you will know well enough just what Shakespeare meant.

And having started upon Shakespeare, here are a few more quotations dealing with falconry. In *Henry VI* Queen Margaret says:

> Believe me, Lords, for flying at the brook,
> I saw not better sport these seven years' day :
> Yet, by your leave, the wind was very high ;
> And, ten to one, old Joan had not gone out.

" For flying at the brook " means for flying at waterfowl or heron. And the reference to old Joan not going out means that the falcon had not been flown.

And King Henry says:

> But what a point, my lord, your falcon made,
> And what a pitch she flew above the rest !—
> To see how God in all his creatures works !
> Yea, man and birds are fain of climbing high.

And then Othello:

> If I do prove her haggard,
> Though that her jesses were my dear heart-strings,
> I'd whistle her off.

It seems that in this context haggard must mean "untameable", though the term in falconry means no more than a passage falcon.

And, finally, one from a play in which one might be excused for not expecting references to sport of this nature. Juliet says:

Hist! Romeo, hist! O for a falconer's voice
To lure this tassel-gentle back again!

And here, of course, tassel is merely Elizabethan tiercel.

So much for Shakespeare, the falconer. Shakespeare was writing at the time when the sport had a great hold on the people, at the time when you might know pretty well a man's status by the hawks he kept. But hawking is a sport with a much longer lineage than that. It goes back far beyond Elizabethan times into the mists of antiquity. It seems probable that hawking originally developed in Thrace, and very early at that, though I have heard that the honour of inventing the sport should go to the Mongols. Be that as it may, hawks were certainly flown in England in Saxon times, and probably earlier than that. Of course, the sport had not then become a science, and it was considerably later when it had advanced to the point at which you knew a man's social status by the hawk he owned. So popular did the sport become that every man, according to his social rank, had a particular sort of hawk assigned to him. The more noble species were reserved for kings and princes and nobles, and this was only right, since these species had as a rule to be imported from abroad, often at great cost. Humble men had to be content with more ordinary species. Thus the peregrine gentle, the gyr-falcon, and the goshawk were reserved for the gentry, the sparrow-hawk and the kestrel for men of more lowly position. In time the sparrow-hawk came to be identified with the Church (but not with bishops, who were nobles), being the "bird of the holy water clerk". The most popular bird was the goshawk, and this was because both the male and female goshawk are birds of considerable bloodthirstiness when in pursuit of their quarry, but are quite remarkably mild and easy to handle. They were, moreover, as they still are, "birds of the hand". That is to say, they were, and are, flown straight from the hand, which they leave with the velocity of a shot from a gun. They have other advantages, too. They do not have to be persuaded to return by means of a lure. A goshawk is a bird that hits or misses, and if it is well trained (and if it is well trained it is affectionate) it will immediately return to the hand after a miss.

A good goshawk regards its master's hand as its home. The goshawk was once the typical hawk of the English country gentleman, a bird to be carried about with one on one's walks abroad. (The falcon gentle, on the other hand, was more nearly allied to the chase, and was usually carried by a mounted man, which, of course, made the whole thing, even in the days of the horse, more of a business.) And, of course, the goshawk was popular because in those days it bred in England, and apparently in considerable numbers.

Hawking became so popular, and so fashionable, that the most stringent laws were passed to protect the eyries and nests, and a very heavy fine or imprisonment was the punishment meted out to those who stole another man's hawk. Henry VII passed such a law. Henry VIII made it a felony to take the king's nestling falcons or the eggs out of a nest, or to capture one of the King's hawks and not to hand it over to one of the royal falconers within ten days. Times change indeed. To-day, though some of the hawks and falcons receive protection, and, indeed, all hawks and falcons are protected for some portion of the year, this protection is purely in theory. In practice the protection laws are not enforced because they are not enforceable.

Hawking reached its greatest popularity, and certainly was most fashionable, during the reign of James I. The Scottish King was very keen on all field sports, and devoted a good deal of his time to hunting the hare with beagles and hawks, and also to flying his hawks at birds. He spent a vast amount of money every year on hawks. Hawking was not a cheap amusement. You can to-day pay a very considerable sum for a pair of guns from a first-class maker, but you will be a fool indeed if you pay the price of a pair of good hawks in Stuart times. Sir Thomas Monson paid £1000 in the reign of James I for a pair of goshawks, and money was money in those days. But earlier than that hawks were worth a king's ransom. One of the Crusader princes was ransomed from the Saracens for twelve Greenland falcons. That must mean that hawking was practised by the Saracens with zest and knowledge, and it must also mean that they knew a Greenland falcon when they saw one. And think what the price of just one Greenland falcon must have been in those days of limited communication.

The decline of falconry commenced with the Restoration. It did not give way at first to the musket and the fowling-piece.

That came about later. The reason for its decline was that it went out of fashion at Court. William III was indifferent, and the Hanoverian kings were not sportsmen. And following the decline came the improvement in firearms, the enclosure of common and open lands, the drainage of the fens, and the destruction of the forests. And the introduction of shot finished it off. It was bound to decline in any case, fashionable or not. The enclosures would have seen to that without the aid of any other factor. But it has never died out, and for that all true sportsmen must be thankful. Still to-day hawks are flown in the English countryside, though not as frequently as I, personally, would like to see, and still to-day the terms that Shakespeare knew are used by falconers. It is not a dying sport; it will never die. But it is moribund, and it will remain moribund. It can never now be more than the hobby of the few, for the country is too enclosed to permit of its being conducted on any scale. All the same, I think that it could be conducted on a somewhat larger scale than is at present the case. It is not a difficult matter to take a hawk alive. It is not a difficult matter to train a hawk. Nor is it expensive. And hawks might be used with advantage by gamekeepers in the exercise of their duties. I should dearly love to see some greater revival of the sport in England.

The hare has only recently been regarded as an animal to shoot. George Markland thought the shooting of hares a crime, and he was expressing the opinion of his time and the opinion commonly held by sportsmen for many years after he was dead. A hundred years after Markland you will find a shooting man excusing the shooting of hares. Captain Richard Lacy published his *The Modern Shooter* in 1842, and I quote from it:

> He who shoots a hare in a good open coursing country must expect reproaches from " the still small voice of conscience ", and no honied compliments from the still louder one of his neighbours; and as for shooting hares on a public coursing ground, or on lands thereto belonging, it is as bad as being a vulpicide in a fox-hunting country, which leaves nothing more to be said. But am I, situated in a closely fenced district, to refrain from shooting hares on my own grounds or where I have permission from others? No ! no ! here, I conceive, rests the distinction betwixt the sporting propriety and impropriety of shooting hares. In countries abounding in small enclosures, thick fences, plantations, and woods, you may run greyhounds after hares but can have no coursing. Unless,

therefore, there be a clever little pack of beagles in the neighbourhood, or a pack of harriers, with a decided paucity of hares—for too many are as inimical to hare-hunting as too few—I should certainly shoot them; at all events occasionally.

Thus Captain Richard Lacy. He is obviously making a case for himself. One might think that he had made a pretty good case for himself. But evidently he did not think that it was going to carry much weight with his friends. Read that last sentence again. Captain Richard Lacy is not at all sure of his ground; he is hedging. "At all events occasionally." That is not a confident man speaking. In his day it was obviously not thought good form to shoot hares under any circumstances.

But then remember Cobbett. You will remember the passage in his *Rural Rides* in which he describes a visit to Netheravon in Wiltshire, and on the edge of Salisbury Plain. He had been told of a strange sight that was to be seen there, and he wanted to see it for himself. His host, Mr. Hicks Beach, showed it to him. " He took us into a wheat stubble close to his paddock; his son took a gallop round, cracking his whip at the same time; the hares (which were very thickly in sight before) started all over the field, ran into a flock like sheep; and we all agreed that the flock did cover an acre of ground."

There you have it. The gun was not intended for the hare. But the farmer must keep the hare within limits. Necessity has thrust the hare upon the gun. For it is only the gun that can keep the hare down when she is intent upon damage to agriculture.

And yet I do not think that one shooting man in a hundred really enjoys shooting hares. I think that most of them would agree with Robbie Burns. Did you know that Scotland's national poet was a shooting man and a shooting poet? But he was. And here are some verses of his, whose title I like particularly:

ON SEEING A WOUNDED HARE LIMP BY ME, WHICH A FELLOW HAD JUST SHOT AT.

> Inhuman man! curse on thy barbarous art,
> And blasted be thy murder-aiming eye;
> May never pity soothe thee with a sigh,
> Nor ever pleasure glad thy cruel heart!
>
> Seek, mangled wretch, some place of wonted rest,
> No more of rest, but now thy dying bed!
> The sheltering rushes whistling o'er thy head,
> The cold earth with thy bloody bosom prest.

Oft as by winding Nith, I, musing, wait
The sober eve, or hail the cheerful dawn,
I'll miss thee sporting o'er the dewy lawn,
And curse the ruffian's aim, and mourn thy hapless fate.

Yes, the trouble about shooting hares is the wounded ones. For a wounded hare is a horrible sight indeed, and a wounded hare cries for all the world like a small child that has been hurt. So that I, personally, hate shooting hares, and will not do so if I can possibly avoid it. And here I am in good company—the company of Eric Parker, the best of all shooting writers and the author of the best of all shooting books, *Shooting Days*. And this is what Mr. Parker has to say about it:

> When I see her, I like to think of her as a hare of the old fairy-tales, going about the world under a spell; or as a hare to be delivered by Moll White the witch, as Moll delivered her from Sir Roger de Coverley's hounds; or as one of St. Monacella's lambs, for whom in Wales peasants prayed, " God and St. Monacella be with thee ! " so that she should escape her pursuers; or a hare such as Boadicea loosed from her robe before her warriors, to see which way the creature of omen would run, and get that way advice from heaven. And so when she crouches flat in the furrow and watches me with her nervous brown eye, or steals soft-footed down the stubble within reach of me and no other, I tell her that she is out of shot altogether or I look the other way.

And I do too. It is not that I object to killing hares—for I do not—it is that I object to shooting them. Yet hares must be shot. For hares must be kept down. That is the only justification for shooting them.

I can find no justification whatever for putting down hares for shooting, and very little for maintaining a good stock simply for the shooting. A good stock of hares in a non-agricultural country is another matter, of course; there is every justification for maintaining such a stock, since it can do comparatively little harm, and is valuable from the food-supply point of view. But to maintain a good stock deliberately in an agricultural country simply for the shooting, simply as an adjunct to the pheasants and partridges, is in my opinion quite unwarranted. It is done, for all that. And it is comparatively easy to do. The keeper has only to remember that hares need a lot of cover. But to maintain such a stock it is necessary, since the hare is a comparatively easy mark, to impose a limit on the number shot each season, and it is also necessary to introduce fresh blood almost every season. Hares can usually be procured from a game farm at a reasonable price, but it is generally better to get them from neighbouring country.

On Salisbury Plain, and elsewhere where hares are plentiful, they are driven. If you are anything of a shot, this is by far the best way of getting rid of them. For hares are not driven fast. A hare only moves fast when she is escaping from imminent danger, and she does not regard a line of beaters as imminent danger, and does not think that she is escaping from anything. So she moves forward cautiously and at a slow pace, since she is not sure what is before, and also because she does not want to go farther than is absolutely necessary. So she should be an easy mark. Yet it is astonishing how frequently she is missed. Too many people take long shots, and long shots more often wound than kill. You will see hares killed by long shots, of course, usually by long shots taken broadside, but such occasions are few and far between. My advice to a young shot would be " never take a long shot at a hare; always make certain ". It is very much better to be sure than sorry; and you are no sportsman if you wound a hare and are not sorry about it. It is very much better to let a hare go than to wound her. Always make certain. For this reason I prefer, if I must shoot hares—and nowadays I never do—to have them driven to me through a hedge. A hare on passing through a hedge always stops and looks around, and, moreover, always sits bolt upright to do so. It is murderously simple. It is not sport. But it is sure. And if it must be done, as it must in certain parts of the country, that is the way I would have it done.

Then there is the hare that comes forward from the beaters when other game is the main object of the day. It is astonishing how soon hares and rabbits do come forward—long before the first pheasant may be expected. These hares at these shoots I always tried not to see—and I have known many others shooting do the same—but it is not always possible to turn the blind eye. And hares make good eating. If some other gun shoots them, I have no objection. I like eating hare. The fact of the matter is that I am afraid of missing the vital spot, and frightened that I shall not miss altogether.

Chapter V

AND STILL MORE WAYS

When I was a-reaping
  Near famed Wantage Town
A girt hare came leaping,
  So sleek an' so brown:
An' me being gifted,
  Like David, to sling,
A pebble I lifted
  An' dropped her at spring.
            Patrick Chalmers.

IF there are more legitimate ways of killing a hare than by hunting her, there are as many illegitimate ways as there are legitimate, and more. The fox has to a very large extent usurped the position of the hare in the eyes of the sporting gentry, but in the eyes of the sporting peasant, who is in many ways an Elizabethan still, the hare remains the supreme beast of the chase. And certainly it is still, and always will be, the most prized quarry of the poacher, other than the professional from the towns, be he farm labourer or moucher or Gypsy. And for the simple reason that a hare is a big animal and carries a lot of meat, and will provide, in one way and another, meals for a week for any normal-sized family.

Now, there are any number of ways in which you can poach a hare. There is many a farm labourer who is as adept as the man in Patrick's poem at casting a stone. I have seen it done several times, and marvelled at the skill in aiming and at the force of the throw. Dangerous men to have in the outfield at a cricket match, if only they could throw a cricket ball as well as they can chuck a stone. But they cannot. The best thrower of a stone I have ever seen was a farm labourer in my village, quite a young fellow and very active (he was killed in North Africa fighting with the Hampshires), who was also a stalwart of the village team, and a good bat.

E   65

I have seen him on two occasions bowl over a hare with a stone, and more than one rabbit has he had that way. But he could not throw a cricket ball any better than the Vicar, and that, as the Vicar will be the first to admit, is not very well. But the poaching of a hare by means of a chucked stone is a casual business, and cannot be regarded seriously. The throw-stick is a different matter. The throw-stick is almost extinct in the English countryside nowadays, but there are still a few men who do use them. The stick is short, fatter at one end than at the other, and with the fat end slightly weighted. The fat end is so shaped that it may be held in the hand with comfort, just as one holds a knobbed cane, and it is thrown so—that is, without changing the position of the stick in the hand. Once thrown, the stick revolves in the air so that it is the weighted end that strikes the target. Tremendous force can be got behind a stick thrown in this manner, and in the hands of an expert it can be a really deadly weapon to man or beast. The last man I saw throw one was a Scottish tinkler, who had a formidable reputation among the wandering folk of the border for his skill with the stick. He was a short, thick-set man with tremendous shoulders, and he threw almost underhand—rather in the same way as Pellew of the 1921 Australian team did from the deep. Those who saw Pellew will remember the almost miraculous way in which he got the ball full-pitch into the wicket-keeper's hands and just over the stumps time after time, with that peculiar half-sideways and half-underhand chuck from the deep-field, and how he would do it the while he was running at full speed. My tinkler threw like that. He would do it while he was walking along, and apparently without aiming. And he rarely missed. The weighted end of the stick struck the hare or rabbit—and I have seen him have both grouse and blackgame in the same way—on the lower half of the body, usually on the forelegs. It did not kill the animal—though I have seen a bird killed outright by a throwing-stick—but it stopped it for long enough to enable the thrower to come up and secure it. The distance up to which this tinkler could be tolerably sure of hitting his mark was 30 yards, and most of the stick-throwers I have known or heard about have preferred a distance of 25 yards, or a little more, rather than a short distance. I suppose this has something to do with the balance of the stick. Some of the Scottish tinklers who still use the stick, but who are not very good at the sudden and apparently unaimed shot, also use dogs. The dogs drive the hares, and the men are so placed that they can get an aimed shot at the hare as she runs. The method of throwing is the same, and the stick hits at or about the forelegs, but it is not so satisfactory a method, for the hare stopped in full flight, as it were, proves too great a temptation for the dogs, and is usually pounced upon before their owner can get on the scene, and that usually means a damaged hare.

While on the subject of Scottish tinklers I may as well deal with the Blue Hare and the methods of poaching it that I have come across. I have not travelled much with the Scottish tinklers, and those with whom I have travelled were not much good at poaching, except for the stick-thrower, and he had few other accomplishments, so that my knowledge of poaching the Blue Hare is not as complete as I could wish.

All the poaching of hares that I witnessed took place in daylight. In my experience the Scottish tinkler, in contrast to his English Gypsy cousin, does not work much at night. The family that I travelled with—it was more than a family, really, for, though they were all closely related, they did not break up on marriage, and so there was a collection of families passing as one—possessed lurchers, and quite well-trained ones, too, and also a couple of Bedlingtons, that were really good poaching dogs where birds were concerned. The family also possessed several light carts. The practice was to drive along a road or lane, and whenever a likely-looking field was seen, one of the dogs would be released from the cart (the dogs travelled in the carts, but were not chained in any way, and the method of release was simply a signal by wave of the arm) and sent into the field. The dog would then begin to range the field rather in the manner of a setter, and if there was a hare in the field it would usually be roused. Instantly the man in the cart would be down, would have a light net out of his pocket, and would set this across a gateway. If you want to see a man move really fast, watch a tinkler doing this. It is no more than a matter of seconds from the moment the lurcher has found his hare to the setting of the net over the gateway, and only a moment or two before the hare is pocketed. The lurcher courses the hare at about half-speed or a little more, and works her towards the gateway. Should she try to turn for the hedge or fence on either side of the field, the dog will put on speed and turn her, and if he cannot do that he will bowl her over and kill. But these dogs are clever, and usually the hare was turned into the gateway, though sometimes it took several turns. Just before she reaches the gateway, the dog puts on full speed, and so dashes her into the net, and his master does the rest. The dog jumps into the cart and rests to get his breath back, and is soon ready for the next course. I remember an afternoon during which I saw seven hares taken in this manner. If the field does not hold a hare the driver of the cart starts to drive on, and at once the dog will leave the field and come running and jump up into the back of the cart while it is moving— an extraordinarily graceful sight.

The Blue Hare, when disturbed, and not turned by dogs, will invariably make for the highest ground in its neighbourhood—for the hill-tops, if there be hill-tops. This peculiarity is not unknown to the tinkler and to those others who poach in Scotland. I have watched tinklers drive a gully with the dogs and put all the hares up the hill, and, so clever were the dogs, to just the spot at which men and women were waiting to receive them. The ground before this drive started did not appear to hold a single hare, but within a few moments of the dogs being put in hares were starting up all over the place, and a good haul was made at the top. A few got through the barrage, and one or two turned back and got away, but most of those that turned back were chopped by the dogs, who had evidently done this sort of thing many times, for they knew just what to expect.

But though the tinklers' dogs are clever, they cannot compare with the dogs used by the English Gypsies. The training is not nearly so thorough, and no trouble is taken over the breeding. Moreover, the Scottish tinkler will use dogs as frequently as bitches, even to the exclusion of bitches on occasion, and that may be taken as a sound indication of the respective merits of the two as poachers.

The art of snaring or trapping wild animals seems to be invested with a certain amount of mystery. It is the art of uncivilised peoples, and we are a civilised people, and so, when we come across a person who is adept in the ways of the savage, we are impressed and slightly awed, and we exaggerate his powers and his knowledge of the wild. But though the average man does do that, it must not be thought that there is not an art in snaring. There is no art in trapping nowadays, for the gin trap can be used by any one who is callous enough, but snaring is an art. It is an art, moreover, the secrets of which are jealously guarded and handed down from

" The Blue Hare . . . will invariably make for the highest ground. . . ."

generation to generation. It has been said that " poaching is a
lost art in Britain ", which it certainly is not, but it might truthfully
be said that snaring is a lost art in Britain, except among certain
poachers.   I have watched many people set snares—and I have set
many snares myself—but I have seen few men that I would call
artists at the job.   I have known some artists, though; three farm
labourers come to mind whenever I think of snaring rabbits, and
when it comes to snaring hares, I can think of some half-dozen
men—four Gypsies and two farm labourers—who stand out head
and shoulders above all the many I have seen trying their skill at
this very difficult business.

It is not a difficult business because the hare is a difficult animal
to snare.   If you know anything about the habits of hares, it is
one of the easiest, perhaps the easiest, of all animals to snare.   But
it is not an easy animal to snare silently.   And if you cannot snare
silently, you might just as well not snare at all from the artistic
point of view.

There is no wild creature in this country that is capable of uttering
so pitiful a cry as the hare, and there are few cries that carry so far,
especially on a still night.   A hare wounded by a shot from a gun
makes the most pitiful of cries, but that is as nothing to the noise
a hare caught in a snare will make.   Many a poacher must have
been caught by the keepers because of the crying of a hare in one
of his snares.   (On the other hand, I have known the keepers to
be lured away from the spot at which poachers were working by
one of their number imitating the cry of a wounded hare some little
distance away.)   So if you would snare hares and have no trouble,
you must learn to do it in such a way that they do not cry out.

A snare is a very simple affair, and can be made in a few minutes.
It consists of a running noose, the end of which terminates in a round
loop or eye.   A piece of strong cord or string is passed through
the eye of the snare and secures it to whatever anchor is selected.
Wire is used for the snare.   There are different qualities of wire,
and you must get the right sort.   Very thin wire is useless, for it
would snap in frosty weather.   A single strand of wire is not
enough.   You need from six to eight strands plaited together,
and there are different ways of doing this.

Any schoolboy can make a snare, and any schoolboy can set a
snare.   There is nothing in the least difficult about either making
or setting.   But managing snares successfully is a very different

matter. To do that requires a long apprenticeship in the green fields, and a very intimate knowledge of the habits of the hare. First of all there is the setting of the snare. You will usually read that the anchor must be driven firmly into the ground. I have even read that a stout peg should be used, and that this should be driven firmly into the ground. Well, you will not catch many hares if you follow that advice. Then there is the question of keeping the noose in the proper place. This is sometimes done by driving a forked piece of wood into the ground to support the straight end of the noose. And then there is the question of the height at which the noose should be suspended. Generally, if the snare is intended for a hare in the open, it is set at about 7 inches from the ground. You can measure the height easily enough and accurately enough by setting it to the level of the thumb raised at right angles to the palm of the hand. There is also some question of the size of the noose. A noose set for hares in the open must be bigger than one set for hares in a hedge. An animal creeping through a hedge pushes a snare up with its feet more often than not. Those are good general rules. But we must return for a moment to the question of driving the holding peg firmly into the ground. This, for hares, is all wrong. A hare snared in anything firm will scream like a child, and will go on screaming until it dies, and every one for a long way round will know just what has happened. A hare caught in something that it can move will rarely scream, but will go on jumping about trying to free itself, and will therefore be all the more quickly spent. There is one other elementary rule about setting a snare: never set it to any fixed object. It is astonishing how frequently I see this rule broken in the country-side nowadays. And I see other rules that are elementary to the good poacher broken every day. A good poacher will never set a snare before dusk, and he will never leave it until daybreak. Yet I can go for a country walk and see snares about quite as often as I can go for a walk and see no snares.

Though the hare is so cunning when hunted, she is, in fact, a creature of habit. Hares have their particular entrances and exits in fields, and they stick to these under almost all circumstances. A hare leaving its form takes no precautions, but goes straight to the particular exit of the field. Returning to the form is a different matter, and the greatest precautions are taken to baffle the scent, many doubles and turns, and finally two very long jumps—anything up to about 18 feet. Of course, this regularity of habit makes the hare a comparatively easy animal to poach. But even so you must know a good deal about hares, and in particular you must have a trained eye for its " trod "—that is, for its track. You must be able to tell the difference between the trod of a hare and the track of a rabbit. Can you? It is not so difficult. A rabbit usually runs straight, a hare rarely does so. Of course, a hare or a rabbit, if it is hunted or terrified, will run wherever it thinks that safety lies, but in the normal course of life the rabbit goes pretty straight, and the hare wanders hither and thither, winding about. But it will follow its favourite winds, just as the rabbit follows its favourite runs. And the trod of a hare is a little broader than the track of a rabbit.

But you must know more than that if you would really make sure of getting your hare as often as possible. You must find the bolt-holes of the hare from the fields. A rabbit jumps over obstacles ; a hare, unless closely pursued, tries to find a way through them. It is a strange idiosyncrasy on the part of an animal that can jump so far and so beautifully, but there it is. A rabbit will leave a field pretty straight ; the exit of a hare is usually diagonal. Once you have learned these things and have learned the signs of them at a glance, then you will be able to start snaring seriously. Fortunately, it takes a long time.

The use of nets takes even longer to learn. In the south of England the only people left who now use nets expertly are, I think, the Gypsies. There are several sorts of nets for hares. There are gate-nets, spout-nets, drop-nets, bag-nets, and just nets. All are made on the same principle as the long net, but all have their especial uses. With the exception of drop-nets and bag-nets, all are used in conjunction with the dogs. I have only once seen the bag-net in operation, and I think that its use must almost have died out. I have never seen the drop-net in operation, and I think that in England it is now no longer used, but I believe that it is still used by one family of Welsh Gypsies, and I am told that it may still be seen in use among the tinklers of Ireland.

The spout-net is used to cover any tunnel exit of a hare from a field. It is not so very much bigger than an ordinary purse-net, but it is much stouter in build. The light gate-net is used for day-light work, and in much the same way as the Scottish tinklers use it. A man driving a light cart along a lane will have in the cart

The mountain hare does not make a " form ".

a couple of dogs, nestling down in the straw and almost invisible, and in his pocket he will have a gate-net. Passing a likely field, he will signal his dogs away, and stop the cart. The dogs will run the field at a great pace, one on each side of it, turn at the top, and work the field down towards the gate, still at a great speed. Any hare in the field is put up, and instantly the dogs course her, closing her in, and finally driving her into the gate and the net that will be there awaiting her. Should she turn and avoid the gate they will turn to course her again, but, though it depends upon the situation of the field and the amount of traffic that is likely to be met with, the owner will usually whistle his dogs off after the first course. And so well trained are they that they will immediately obey the whistle. If no hare is put up, then the owner will get back into his cart and the dogs will jump up after him, and the same thing will be tried at another field. The system is the same as in Scotland, but always two dogs are used, and they work the field more thoroughly and more quickly.

Netting at night is done for rabbits and hares. Netting rabbits with a net and the aid of two intelligent dogs is an easy business, particularly if you do not want too many rabbits. And rabbits are easy things to conceal. A man can carry two, one down each trouser-leg, and swing along so that you would not guess his burden. But taking hares with just two dogs, a net and a man is a different business altogether. The net is fixed at the gateway to the field, and the man stands by to do the necessary as soon as the animal is in the net. The difficulty comes in training the dogs to turn the hare into the net, for the hare, as I have already pointed out, is a conservative animal and has its own favourite exits from a field, and these are unlikely to include the gate. This means that there must be some reconnaissance beforehand to find the hare's way in and way out. It is the way out that matters, for hares will invariably leave a field by the same exit if allowed to do so, though they are not by any means so particular about the way in. It might seem that the obvious thing to do is to net this exit, and, of course, this is done when the exit is in a good place for the man's own getaway. But the occasions on which it is are remarkably few—the exit is usually in a corner, and a corner is not a good place to be caught in. So the net is set at the gate. Then one dog is placed at the hare's exit (where he will wait patiently, knowing full well what he has to do),

and the other dog is taken round the field to the side opposite the
exit and as nearly as possible at the furthermost extremity consistent
with this from the gate. The man then returns to the gate, and
when he is ready gives a low whistle. The dog at the exit remains
steady, but the other enters the field and puts up the hare. The
hare goes for its exit, finds it barred, turns, and is instantly between
two fires, and it does not take two good dogs long to turn it into
the gate. Here another difficulty arises, for it is difficult to train
two excited dogs not to follow a hunted hare into the net in the dark
and kill it. The man must do the killing; it saves the net. But I
have seen some wonderfully well-trained dogs, and met some men
expert at the art of killing a hare so quickly that it has not time to
scream. By the way, a hare hunted by dogs will hardly ever
scream—the hunt will be silent enough, for a poacher's dogs know
better than to yelp—but, once in the net, there will be screams
enough to rouse the dead if the man at the gate is not very quick
indeed.

Piping a hare is an art that is almost dead in England. I have
seen it done in Hampshire once or twice, and I have watched a real
expert at the job in Wales. Both men were very old, and I know
of no young men who practise the art, so it is probably dying out,
and may be extinct when these two pass on. But I hope not.

There has been some controversy about piping hares. In the
reign of Richard II a law was passed prohibiting the use by un-
authorised persons of dogs for hunting, ferrets, nets, hare-pipes,
or other engines to take or destroy hares. And again in the reign
of James I we find a law enacting that any person who should take
or destroy a hare by means of a hare-pipe or cord or any such
instrument should pay a fine of twenty shillings. There were
similar laws in the reigns of Charles II, and William and Mary,
and Anne, and the word hare-pipe does not disappear from the
statute-book until 1831, when the Game Act came into force.

Most people think that the hare-pipe is from the context some
sort of trap or snare—something on the lines of a wild-fowl decoy,
which was placed in the exits from fields and so on, just as the
ordinary snare or net is used to-day. Harting, however, in *The
Gun at Home and Abroad*, thinks that it may have referred to a call
to attract hares. So great an authority as Eric Parker disagrees
with him, and plumps in favour of the snare or trap in the sense of
the wild-fowl decoy. I do not know what the meaning of the

word in the old laws was, but I do know that the men who can still call hares call it " piping " hares, and not " calling " hares, and I have never heard any form of trap or snare for hares called a pipe.   Now, ancient words linger on in the country and among country folk, and if there had been, as late as the reign of Queen Anne, a form of trap or snare for hares known as a hare-pipe it is, I think, pretty certain that the word would still be in use somewhere in the British Isles.   I am quite sure that it is not.   But the word is in use still for the call.   And so I am of the opinion that Harting was right, and that the old, illegal hare-pipe was a form of call.

The hare-pipes I have seen have been made of plaited grass. They are very short, and across the end is placed a piece of rush. This is loose, and is held in place by the breath of the user as it is sucked in.   The sound made is a faint squealing—really very faint— but it is effective, for I have seen hares brought up by the caller, and knocked off by a well-directed stone from a catapult by the caller's companion.   I have tried to use a pipe, but I cannot make any sound at all on one.   I have also tried to make one, but without success.

Finally there is the easiest method of taking hares of all the many methods.   This is the taking of the hare in its form in broad daylight with the bare hands.   It may sound easy or incredible: it depends upon how much you know of the ways of hares.   To most people it will sound incredible.   But if you know the literature of the roads, and if you remember some of the writings of the men who were interested in more than the highroad of sport, you will know that it has been known for a very long time that there are certain men who can do this seemingly impossible thing.   You will find mention of it in St. John and in Chapman, for example. And actually it is astonishingly easy to do.   Even I can (more or less) do it.   And I know men who can do it pretty well every time that they try.

I have written before about this taking of the hare in its form with the bare hands in broad daylight.   Mr. Punch's Learned Clerk, reviewing the book in question, complained somewhat bitterly (but, then, food was scarce in those days) that I had deliberately refused to instruct my readers in the art.   I risk more than a complaint this time, I know, but I still refuse.   It is too easy.

Chapter VI

THOSE THAT POACH

When I was bound apprentice in famous Lincolnshire,
Full well I served my master for more than seven year,
Till I took up to poaching, as you shall quickly hear:
O! 'tis my delight on a shiny night
In the season of the year!
Traditional.

THERE are more ways of killing a cat than drowning it in milk. And there are more ways of killing hares than those that appear in the text-books.

A vast number of words have been written about poaching and poachers. Ever since there has been writing about sport—about preserved sport, that is—there has been writing about poaching and poachers. There has been some sensible writing on the subject, but it needs looking for. There has been a great deal of nonsense written also, and this, unfortunately, needs no looking for. This last section of poaching literature can be divided into two classes: that condemning the poacher out of hand and painting him a great deal blacker than he really is; and that sympathising with him. There has, indeed, been a lot of flapdoodle written about the poacher and his activities.

Sir Peter Jeffrey Mackie, in *The Keeper's Book*, has this to say of the poacher:

> The twentieth-century poacher, taking him " by and large ", is an ill-conditioned, lazy, drunken, and slinking scoundrel, an enemy to law and order, without a particle of true sportsmanlike feeling in his veins. As a class, poachers are a set of hardened criminals, careless of everything but their own besotted lives. The occasional

poacher is a much rarer bird, and is the uncurbed expression of the natural poaching tendency which exists in human nature. He may be a farmhand, a village loon, or even a medical student home for the vacation; but whatever he may be, he is, in the majority of cases, an amateur and not so dangerous as his professional brother, who is a cast-off from honest trades—a grain in the lower sediment of society. He is the friend of no man and an enemy to most, and, in the majority of cases, will be found an arrant coward. Remarkably ignorant on most questions, he is terribly acute on all matters affecting the poaching of game, and coward though he be, may be ready at a pinch to get rid of another life rather than risk his own.

Against that you can set the sympathetic approach of, say, Charles Kingsley. Do you remember his poem, *The Outlaw*?

When first I stirred in your side, mither, ye ken full well
How you lay all night up among the deer out on the open fell;
And so it was that I won the heart to wander far and near,
Caring neither for land nor lassie, but the bonnie dun deer.

Yet I am not a losel and idle, mither, nor a thief that steals;
I do but hunt God's cattle, upon God's ain hills;
For no man buys and sells the deer, and the bonnie fells are free
To a belted knight with hawk on hand, and a gangrel loon like me.

So I'm off and away to the muirs, mither, to hunt the deer,
Ranging far frae frowning faces, and the douce folk here;
Crawling up through burn and bracken, louping down the screes,
Looking out frae craig and headland, drinking up the simmer breeze.

Oh, the wafts o' heather honey, and the music o' the brae,
As I watch the great harts feeding nearer, nearer a' the day,
Oh, to hark the eagle screaming, sweeping, ringing round the sky—
That's a bonnier life than stumbling ower the muck to colt and kye.

And when I'm taen and hangit, mither, a brittling o' my deer,
Ye'll no leave your bairn to the corbie craws, to dangle in the air!
But ye'll send up my twa douce brethren, and ye'll steal me frae the tree,
And bury me up on the brown, brown muirs, where I aye looed to be.

Ye'll bury me 'twixt the brae and the burn, in a glen far away,
Where I may hear the heathcocks craw, and the great harts bray;
And gin my ghaist can walk, mither, I'll go glowering at the sky
The livelong night on the black hillsides where the dun deer lie.

You can take your choice. In the days of which Kingsley's poem was written there may well have been Highland poachers such as that. There may even be some to-day; but there will be very few—very few indeed. Mackie's description of poachers, however, is nonsense, and odious nonsense at that. His book, of course, was written for landowners, and through them for game-keepers. That must be remembered. It is propaganda. The picture is overdrawn—so overdrawn that one is sure that its author can have had no personal experience of poaching and can have known no poachers personally. Either he drew on his imagination for the purpose of building up a case for his readers, or he relied on second-hand information from imaginative informants and did not trouble, or did not wish, to check it for accuracy. Be that as it may, it is a false picture.

It is as foolish to paint a romantic picture of the poacher as it is to paint a romantic picture of any man, be he poacher or poet, politician or pimp. It is as ridiculous to call all poachers cowards and drunkards and slinking scoundrels as it is to call all soldiers heroes. All men are pretty much the same when you take their clothes off.

But there are degrees in all men. Some soldiers are braver than others, some are smarter. Some politicians tell the truth sometimes. There were even degrees among highwaymen: from the common footpad to the Beau Brocade. And so it is with poachers.

Most landowners and most sportsmen—due in no small measure, probably, to the influence of Sir Peter Jeffrey Mackie and *The Keeper's Book*—seem to think that poachers are a class apart, a comparatively small class composed of idle, good-for-nothing fellows. Nothing could be further from the truth. Poaching is common—indeed, prevalent—throughout the countryside, and is not confined to good-for-nothings nor, for the matter of that, to the working or labouring or any other class.

I think that, roughly speaking, poachers may be divided into five groups:

(1) Bandits.
(2) Gang poachers.
(3) Poacher's loafers.
(4) Privileged poachers.
(5) Poachers.

The numbers in each of the first three groups are, I think, small. The numbers in each of the last two are enormous. The members of each of the first three groups are definitely criminals—that is,

consciously dishonest men, who, if they were not poachers, would
be burglars or criminals of some sort. Most of the members of
the last two groups are no more dishonest than the rest of us.

Banditry is little concerned with game. It is a comparatively
new phenomenon. I do not know when it first began in this
country—probably a long time ago—but on any sort of an organised
scale probably not earlier than 1930. There is nothing clever about
it. It is nothing less (and nothing more) than ruthless and highly
organised robbery. The men who carry it out are, I believe, all
townsmen, and the results of the night's work are sold in the big
towns. The raids of townsmen used to be most prevalent in the
neighbourhood of the mining and industrial towns. The gangs
used to be composed of four or five men armed with shot-guns,
who would raid the coverts, fire a score of shots at roosting pheasants
as they might be seen dimly outlined against the night sky, pick up
a dozen birds if they were lucky, and make off in a car or a trap.
I do not know if these men sold the proceeds of a raid (I imagine
not, for a good night's work would not have brought them more
than ten shillings or so—say, two shillings apiece), and I think
that it was largely a question of excitement coupled with a desire
for a change of diet. All the same, such men were usually ready
for a fight, and the mining fraternity, at least, made tough opponents
for any keeper and his assistants. That sort of thing, of course,
still goes on. Indeed, it increased a great deal with the slump.
The industrial areas of Britain were very badly hit by the slump,
and a man with a wife and family did not find it easy to feed them
on the dole, with prices rising. That aspect of poaching in the
neighbourhood of industrial towns during the slump was not
sufficiently realised, if it was realised at all, by those who did not
have to exist on the dole. But it was the slump years that taught
another type of man that there was something to be had in the
woods and hedgerows. The old poaching gang gave place to, or,
at least, was superseded by, the criminal gang, organised on a much
larger scale, and with all the background organisation of the criminal
gang of the town—the scouts, the fences, and so on. These men,
too, were ready for a fight, and very much more prepared to risk
facing a charge of manslaughter. Nor did they confine their
attentions to game. Just before the outbreak of war this banditry
was beginning to become serious. There were one or two large-
scale raids on poultry farms, once or twice cattle were stolen, and

at least once sheep and pigs were taken. During the war, with the added incentive of the Black Market, this sort of thing increased quite a bit. In particular, poultry-thieving became much more common, since it became much more profitable. There were a number of cases of cattle-rustling, and several cases of the disappearance of sheep. In more than one instance there was evidence that sheep had been slaughtered in the fields. This sort of thing naturally took the place of raids upon game stocks. Rabbits, with the attentions of the War Agricultural Executive Committees focused upon them, became too scarce to justify an expedition from town, pheasants were no longer enclosed in the rearing-fields, partridges could not in any case be secured in sufficient numbers to warrant a special journey. Thus farm stocks became the chief objective, and just before Christmas, in particular, these raids became really serious and widespread. The raiders were the shock troops of the Black Market. But prior to the war some attention had been paid to game stocks. These raids were extremely difficult to stop or to deal with in any way. The men came in high-powered cars, did their job quickly, and departed at high speed. There were always a number of men, they were armed, they were prepared for rough stuff, and they were by no means averse to using physical violence, by no means averse to firing, if interfered with. They were rarely interfered with. That they had local information as to the topography, the numbers of gamekeepers and so forth is beyond doubt. It was fortunate that there were never many of these motor-borne bandits at work, but they were, from the gamekeepers' point of view, and indeed from that of the countryman generally, a most disturbing phenomenon. Presumably there will be a great diminution in their numbers with the return to settled conditions and the decrease in the Black Market, but should there be another slump, gamekeepers may look out for trouble, for the precedent has been set.

But it is wrong to call these gangs poaching gangs. They are analogous to the smash-and-grab raiders of the towns. They are a purely urban manifestation, a further and most unpleasant example of the spread of the town into the countryside.

The poaching gang is quite different. It is a rural growth, and it is very much older than the Game Act. Indeed, it is as old as the history of England. Our Norman kings took severe measures to stamp out the poaching gangs, and it is their laws that are most

F

familiar to the average Englishman. But even before the coming
of the Normans and their harsh game laws our Saxon kings had
been troubled by poaching gangs. Evidence of this and of the
drastic steps they took to stop such activities occasionally comes
to light. For example, a recent excavation near Stockbridge in
Hampshire disclosed a communal burial of a number of young
men and one old one. All had been beheaded. There were not
enough of them to suggest that they had been victims of a battle,
and in any case all the casualties in a battle would not have been
beheaded. This was a mass execution. There was no town in
the neighbourhood in those days, but there was a village, and the
view that these men had been caught raiding the King's game,
and for the crime summarily executed on the hill near their village
as a warning to others, is inescapable. From that day to this the
poaching gang has survived everywhere.

The poaching gang have this in common with the motor-borne
bandit: that the result of their night's work is sold. The idea
that these men poach for the love of sport or in order to get food
to eat (and that is the idea that is commonly held) is wrong. They
do not. They poach for money. There is only a difference in
degree between their poaching and burglary.

Poaching gangs are usually small. A gang of more than half
a dozen men is a large gang. Each gang works a definite and well-
defined area which the members know intimately. Infringement
of the boundaries of this area is certain sooner or later to lead to
trouble with the neighbouring gang, and since the last thing the
gangs want is trouble between themselves, the boundaries are
usually rigidly observed. But the areas covered are sometimes
quite large. Unlike the motor-borne bandit gang, poaching
gangs are, in my experience, invariably made up of countrymen.
They may live and work (and usually do) in small country towns—
it is most uncommon to find a member of a poaching gang living
in a small village, and it is most uncommon to find a farm labourer
or a man working right in the country who is a member of one of
these gangs—but they are countrymen, with country knowledge,
and the ways of the country deep in their blood. I have been at
pains on several occasions to enquire into the family history of
members of poaching gangs caught and convicted. In almost
every case they have been men who have migrated from the land
to some job in a small country town or a large village—men forced

off the land by economic conditions—or they have been the sons or grandsons of farm labourers. In only two cases have I come across men who have not had this country background. In one case the man was a draper's assistant, to all appearances a highly respectable and rather smug individual. He was a man of superior intelligence and considerable organising ability, and he was beyond doubt the brains of his gang. He was a Londoner, and so far as I could discover had had no connection with the country until he came to the small market town in which he lived at the time of his conviction to take up the chief assistant's job at the chief drapery establishment. How he came to join up with the local poachers I never discovered, but it was certainly not love of sport that made him do so. It was love of money. In the other case the man was a cobbler, the son of a sergeant in the Metropolitan Police and the grandson of a Midland town bricklayer; and on his mother's side, too, there was a history of townsfolk. As far back as it was possible to trace this man's family there was not a vestige of country blood. Why he came to the small Hampshire market town, I do not know. All his previous existence had been in London, and he had married the daughter of an East-End docker. He had two previous convictions for burglary. Twenty-two other convicted poachers, all members of poaching gangs, whose histories so far as I was able I investigated, were countrymen or countrymen but slightly removed. Eleven were former farm workers, who had left the land " to better " themselves; seven were the sons of farm labourers who had come to work in the towns because of the depressed conditions in agriculture; four were the grandsons of farm labourers. All were in steady employment, but with three exceptions they had what I imagine were poorly paid jobs. The three exceptions were a man who had a good job as a chauffeur in a private household; a man who was employed by the local council; and a man who was a gardener in a private household, had a cottage rent free and was drawing good money. Seventeen of the twenty-two were married, and twelve of them had families. Eighteen of the twenty-two had suffered some period of unemployment. But poorly paid jobs and periods of unemployment are not sufficient in themselves to make men members of poaching gangs. There are many poorly paid jobs in the country, and a disgracefully high proportion of our male population before the war had experienced periods, and long periods, of unemployment. Furthermore, some of these men had not experienced periods of unemployment, and none of them had experienced really long periods, and some did hold good and reasonably well-paid jobs. No, all these men were after money, and did not mind how they got it. They were all dishonest men, criminals—petty criminals maybe, but criminals for all that.

But though they were criminals, they certainly did not fit Sir Peter Jeffrey Mackie's description of a poacher. Not one of them was " ill-conditioned, lazy, drunken ". They were all scoundrels, but not one could truthfully be described as a " slinking scoundrel ". Indeed, it may be taken as a fact that a man who is out of condition will not be a real poacher—the profession (if it may be dignified by such a title) demands a high standard of physical fitness. And it may also be taken as a fact that a drunkard will not be a poacher. I have known a good many poachers of one sort and another, and I have not yet met one who was a drunkard. Most of them have, in fact, been very light drinkers.

There is one other fact about the poaching gang, and it holds true for most types of poacher, which Sir Peter Jeffrey Mackie forgot to mention (or perhaps he did not know it), and that is that poachers are almost always men in jobs. Unemployed men do do a bit of poaching, of course, but the real professionals are men in jobs. And the reason, to anyone who really knows the country and country ways, is not far to seek.

Once in a poaching gang, it is very difficult to get out. The success or failure of the gang depends largely upon strict secrecy. A chance word dropped in a pub or within earshot of others at a street corner may mean capture and conviction. The members are not bound together by any ties of loyalty, but by fear, and each member watches the other jealously during off-duty hours. During the actual raid they are, of course, held together by the job in hand and the excitement. And the excitement—for it is an exciting life (I have this on more than one excellent authority)—grows rather than diminishes. The thrill of working secretly in the dark, the thrill of setting snares in the broad daylight of a Sunday, the thrill of evading keepers, the thrill of hunting—these are thrills that become more and more difficult to conquer. Furthermore, there is the thrill of success and the pleasure of having more money in one's pocket than that earned at a workaday job. Thrills, success, suspicion: these make up the life of a member of a poaching gang.

But the intervals of high excitement compensate for the periods of doubt and suspicion and jealous watchfulness. I suppose that the same is true of those urban forms of gang poaching—burglary, smash-and-grab and so forth. And just as these urban industries could not exist without a market, so the poaching gang could not exist without a market. The burglar is not interested in jewellery as such; the smash-and-grab merchant does not push in a window because he collects diamond rings as a stamp collector collects stamps. So with a member of a poaching gang. He has no interest in rabbits or pheasants or partridges as such. He does not want them for his larder. He is interested only in the money they bring in.

I have no information as to the markets, but it is evident that there must be in many (probably in all) country towns a ready sale for poached game, since the hauls, particularly of rabbits, are sometimes large. Presumably the sale is to restaurants, hotels, shops, public-houses, and so forth. No doubt there are proprietors of such places who do not worry much about where the stuff comes from so long as it comes and is good, but I imagine that the number of such men—men willing to buy obviously stolen stuff—must be very limited in small country towns. It seems evident that just as there are fences for stolen property in the cities, so there must be fences for poached game in the small country towns. They would, I think, be men who run a perfectly sound and honest business, wholesale or retail, in game, poultry and so on. It would be absolutely essential to have a proper " cover " in a small country town. But so far as I know there has not yet been a case in which such a man has been caught and convicted. Which speaks well for the " cover ".

The members of poaching gangs are frequently—but by no means always—known to the gamekeepers of the area they work. But knowing a poacher and catching a poacher are two very different things. Occasionally one reads of a fight between poachers and gamekeepers; occasionally one reads of the capture and conviction of a whole gang of poachers. But such successes are rare—very rare when one remembers that the gang will be at work pretty regularly throughout the year. Poaching gangs will not fight if they can possibly avoid doing so, but a poaching gang is an unknown quantity—it probably will not show fight, but it might. And a gang of, say, half a dozen strong, fit, possibly armed, and certainly desperate, men is not an easy proposition, and gamekeepers working single-handed or with one assistant have but little chance of bringing such a party to book. It has been done, of course. I know of one instance when, in the Winchester neighbourhood, a single-handed gamekeeper, a man of over sixty, secured the whole of a gang of four. But when a capture is made it is more usually the capture of a single member of the gang, and he will not give his fellows away.

The poaching gang is neither so wholesale nor so ruthless in its methods as the gang of motor-borne bandits, but it is a severe enough test for any gamekeeper. It must not be thought, however, that the activities of poaching gangs are confined to the taking of game. That is far from the truth. They will raid poultry if they think they can get away with it and know of a market. And they will raid gardens for the fruit or vegetables and, in season, if there is a demand, for the rarer flowers. Anything that is saleable is grist to their mill.

Some may employ a car, but this is most unusual. It is more usual for the members of the gang to come to the scene of operations on foot or on a bicycle. A car is all right for those who come from a distance, but in the country a car is a definite handicap, for all the cars for several miles around will be known. The criminal in the country, working in a confined area with a small population, but a population of very observant people, works under greater handicaps than his cousin of the big towns.

Snares, traps, nets, ferrets, dogs, guns—these are the weapons of the poaching gang, and in their use, and particularly in the use of the long net, they are expert. But they are not nearly so clever as they are popularly supposed to be. Certainly they are not nearly so clever as some other types of poachers. There is nothing particularly clever about setting a snare or a trap; and there is nothing particularly clever about using ferrets if there are enough of you to do so. The use of the long net at night does require considerable skill—skill as opposed to cleverness—but there is, taken all in all, nothing so very wonderful about the work of a poaching gang. And their dogs are dolts indeed compared to the dogs of some I know. Certainly there is nothing about the work of a poaching gang which is not known to every gamekeeper worthy the name, nothing which a competent gamekeeper could not overcome—if there were sufficient gamekeepers. There are not sufficient gamekeepers, and there never will be. It is this—

the lack of a sufficient force of gamekeepers—coupled with the element of surprise and the comparatively large area over which a gang can work, that accounts for the considerable and consistent success of the poaching gang.

Third on my list was the poacher's loafer. And he must be considered in relation to the poaching gang, for his work is closely connected with theirs. Poacher's loafers are few and far between, and exist, generally speaking, only in those districts in which there is plenty of game preservation and which are worked by two or more poaching gangs. Certainly there are many districts in Britain where the poacher's loafer is quite unknown. " Poacher's loafer ", by the way, is a misleading term, for the man does not work for poachers at all. A poacher's loafer is a man who lives by poaching, but does not actually do any poaching. A loafer: it sounds a lovely, easy, idle job. It is nothing of the sort. It is, as a matter of fact, quite a dangerous job. For a loafer is a man who watches poachers very closely and then robs them of their haul. He keeps the gang or gangs that work his own locality under observation. He must know them all, of course, but he must take great care not to be known to them as a loafer. A loafer can work only so long as he is not known as a loafer by the men upon whom he preys. Once known, he will not loaf any more; quite likely he will not do any active work any more. Accidents, not fatal accidents, have been known in the country before now.

Not only must a loafer know all the members of the gang or gangs operating in his district, he must know the district even more intimately than they do. He must know where and how they work, and where they will attempt poaching under certain conditions, usually weather conditions. And very often—generally, in fact—he must be on the spot before they are. For example, suppose the gang decide to line a fence or two with snares (a common enough practice) and to come back later on to pick up the catch—the loafer goes along the line of snares before they do come back and helps himself to what he wants or to as much as he can carry without too great a risk of detection. Similarly, he will know when the gang are likely to attempt long netting, and where, and he will be able to make a pretty accurate estimate of the probable haul (you *can* estimate these things pretty accurately if you know how), and he will have formed a good idea as to whether the haul is likely to be too big to move in one journey or not. If it is too big for one journey, he knows that the gang will cache part of it, and he will be on hand to see where it is hidden. It will not be there when they return to fetch it, for the loafer will have shifted it, to remove later at his leisure.

If the loafer is a real master at his job, the gang will blame the gamekeepers for their losses, and the gamekeepers will not know that he exists. If he is not a real master at his job, he will probably be known to the gamekeepers. But knowing a loafer is a very different matter from dealing with a loafer. For one thing, the loafer, of course, makes as careful a study of the habits of the local gamekeepers as he does of the members of the gangs. For another, he never carries any poaching tackle on his person. He is some-times caught under suspicious circumstances, but even then it is not easy to bring a case against him.

Occasionally a loafer will do more than prey upon the hauls of a gang. I know of a case in which a loafer removed several hundred yards of long netting set by a gang of poachers—having deliberately disturbed the men just before they settled down to work—and then sold it to a keeper at a very cut price. I saw the netting. It was good netting; almost brand new.

Loafers are men of infinite resource and cunning. A very small slip will mean the end of loafing, if it also does not entail a nasty beating up on some dark night. Circumspection means quite a good living. The results of loafing are, of course, sold—very probably to the same fence that deals with the hauls of the gang—and a successful loafer can do well robbing the robbers. He will do some honest work as well. He must do a certain amount of honest work, sufficient at least to account for his existence in a community where everybody's business is known, for if he did not he would immediately become an object for suspicion. But since much of his time has necessarily to be spent in spying, a full-time job is out of the question.

Jobbing gardening is a favourite occupation with loafers.

Chapter VII

PRIVILEGED POACHERS

On the First of September, one Sunday morn,
I shot a hen pheasant in standing corn
Without a licence.   Contrive who can
Such a cluster of crimes against God and Man!
Richard Monckton, 1st Lord Houghton.

GANG poachers and loafers are professionals.   They belong
to a distinctive type.   They are, it is often said, men lacking
the qualities that go to the making of a conscientious and
industrious workman.   That is, however, a distorted view.   It is
not, in my opinion, a question of the qualities that they lack that
distinguishes them from other men of their station, but rather that
they have an additional quality or two.   They are men of restless
spirit, men with the love of adventure strong within them.   But,
above all, they are men with a natural tendency to crime.   The
fourth class—the privileged poacher; and this is a very large class
indeed—is scarcely ever a man with a tendency to crime, and but
few of them are men of restless spirit.   A small section of them
poach deliberately and know that they are poaching, relying on
various factors to get them away without trouble.   The rest—the
vast majority—just poach and break the Game Laws, right, left,
and centre, all the while, and do not consider that they are doing
any wrong.   And these are the men who are usually most harsh
in their judgement and treatment of poachers.

Let us consider the small section first.   They own motor-cars.
They are well dressed.   They have good jobs in towns.   They are
generally men of reputable social position.   They like going for a

drive of a Sunday morning, and they take a gun in the car.   More
often than not they have omitted to take out a licence.   They take
their drive by quiet roads and lanes.   And they will stop the car
and brown any covey sitting within forty yards of the road.   They
will kill one bird, just possibly two, but they will wound half of
the covey.   If there is no one about they will collect the dead and
drive on to do the same thing a couple of miles farther on.   They
may do so six times of a morning and get six birds, and a rabbit or
two.   They are hardly ever caught; and when they are caught
they are not dealt with with sufficient severity.   They are riff-raff,
no more.   Give me the poacher proper every time.

The vast majority are not riff-raff.   They break the Game Laws
as often—probably, taking the country as a whole, more often—
as do true poachers.   (It is a mistake to think, as Mackie evidently
did, and as the majority of Justices do, that the Game Laws are
broken only by poachers, and that all poachers are members of
what have been described as " the lower orders ".)   But they are
not criminals.   They are obstinate and selfish and jealous.   They
are poachers.   But they are not criminals.

There are people—a considerable number of people—who hold
that the occupation of land should carry with it the unqualified right
to shoot any wild creatures that may be found upon it.   Viewed
in certain lights, that is a reasonable enough opinion, too.   From
the point of view of maintaining a stock of game, however, there is
nothing that can be said in its favour.

Such a system is already in force in some districts owing to the
break up of the big estates, and in these districts the game—or at
least the pheasant—has virtually been exterminated.   Especially
is this so in the remote parts of the West Country.   Here the newly
acquired right to shoot has led to excessive shooting, and little or
no attempt at preservation.   The idea is that the bird is there to be
shot, and if the occupier does not shoot it pretty quickly, then his
neighbour will.   Though farmers are invariably most helpful to
each other in times of stress—aiding each other at threshing and
so forth—this spirit of co-operation does not extend to the shooting.
Far from it: even though pheasants are scarce—very scarce indeed
in some places—a man will, regularly, shoot off his hen birds at
the end of the season.   He knows that if he does not do so they
will sooner or later stray across his boundary to be promptly shot
by his neighbour.   Equally in the few cases in which men do make

some attempt at preserving a few birds, they will shoot as many as possible the moment the law allows them to do so, in order to prevent any from straggling over the boundary for the benefit of their neighbours. This spirit of competition has become so keen that men no longer wait for the legal opening of the shooting season. The pheasant-shooting season opens on 1st October. It is quite safe to say that over large areas of the West Country more pheasants are shot before 1st October than are shot after. It is a question of shooting them early or not shooting them at all. Furthermore, they are shot more often than not on the ten-shilling licence. There is a verse at the head of this chapter. But that was written a long time ago.

From the point of view of maintaining a stock of game, and particularly a stock of pheasants, it will be seen that there is nothing that can be said in favour of granting to the occupier the unqualified right to the shooting. Yet there are many people, and country people at that, who, while well aware of the probable result, hold strongly that the occupier of the land should have the unqualified right to the shooting—and base their argument on the pheasant.

Now, the pheasant is a bird of two aspects, both economic. To the shooting man it is an asset; to the farmer it is a liability. The shooting man too frequently does not see, or does not appreciate, or does not want to see, the damage the pheasant does. The farmer does see the damage. No doubt the pheasant's capacity for inflicting damage is often exaggerated. But, while a few pheasants do not do sufficient damage to worry about, there can be no doubt at all that pheasants in large numbers do do a very considerable amount of damage to agriculture. Where the landlord exercises his right to the shooting, this does not matter much. Very few tenant farmers—I have yet to meet one—resent the landlord's right to shoot or resent the landlord's pheasants. They accept the birds as one of the conditions, albeit one of the less favourable conditions, of the farm. They accept such loss of grain as there may be as part of the rent. The traditional rights of the owner of the soil are still largely recognised by country folk. The feudal spirit, thank God, is not yet wholly dead in Britain.

It is when the landlord allows his rights to pass to a third party that feeling arises. If I have yet to meet a tenant farmer who resents the landlord's birds or the landlord's right to shoot over his land, I have yet to meet a tenant farmer who does not think (though some of them are chary of saying so outright) that should the landlord for any reason fail to exercise his rights, those rights without qualification should automatically pass to the occupier. It is, in my experience, a unanimous opinion.

And it is not a question wholly of damage. It is not even a question of pheasants. The tenant farmer will always maintain that it is. He will go farther than that; he will maintain that he supports the pheasants for some damned outsider to come and shoot. This is the stock argument, but it is not quite so devastating an argument as it appears at first sight. For if there are a large number of pheasants, they are almost certainly artificially produced, hand-reared birds, and if there are not a large number of pheasants, the amount of damage done is insignificant. A man rearing large numbers of pheasants must look after them carefully. He must give them plenty of artificial food, for it is quite certain that there will not be enough food on the fields to support a large stock, and without artificial feeding the birds will stray. Furthermore, all the time the farmer's crops are growing the young birds will mostly be fed at their coops, and when they are at last released to wander, the grain they pick up on the fields, in competition with the rooks and wood-pigeons, is mostly waste. Again, in the early winter months artificial feeding on a most liberal scale is necessary to keep them in the coverts. While I am sure that large numbers of artificially reared birds do do a considerable amount of damage to the farmer, there can be no doubt at all that he does not bear the major part of their maintenance. He will insist that he does, all the same. He will do so even if there are only a few birds on his land.

It is, in fact, not a question of damage or of pheasants. It is something much more complex, something going deep down to the roots of the farmer's being, something wrapped up with the soil and heritage and feudal rights. Social status, too, has something to do with it. And if the shooting tenant—and it does not matter in the least how wealthy he is; money has nothing at all to do with it—is of less exalted social standing (which in this case is a matter of breeding; no more, no less) than the landlord, then the position is aggravated. Even in these days, when we are all being standardised at a low and humdrum level, breeding counts for more than titles or money in the country and among country folk. And if the shooting rights have been let to a syndicate, then indeed does

" Artificial feeding . . . is necessary to keep them in the coverts."

the farmer feel aggrieved. I do not know that in this case social status has so much to do with it. No matter what the social status of the individual members of the syndicate, the farmers over whose land they shoot will feel aggrieved, sometimes bitterly aggrieved. It is the fact that some half-dozen or so men are enjoying what should be the privilege of one man that causes the feeling. Even should these men (as is most frequently the case in my neighbourhood) live in the district and be personally known to every one in the district, that will not be sufficient to kill the feeling, though it may do something to allay it. But should the syndicate be made up, as is too frequently the case, of men living and working at a distance, and coming down only to shoot—using, as I have heard it put by a farmer, the place as "a ruddy convenience"—then feeling is heightened, and the occupier behaves accordingly. Absentee landlords are rarely popular, though they may be exceptionally good landlords and personally nice and gentle men. Absentee syndicates are invariably unpopular.

And what does the tenant farmer do? He poaches. He would not call it that, of course. And he would be most irate if he found someone helping himself to his rabbits. Nevertheless, that is what he does. I do not know how much poaching is done by tenant farmers when the landlord exercises the shooting rights. It depends, no doubt, a good deal on the landlord. But I do know that there is a certain amount of illicit shooting by tenant farmers even when the landlord does exercise the shooting rights and is highly regarded by his tenants. I have come across several such cases myself. Often, I think, the farmer does not realise that he is poaching, or, if he once did realise it, has come to regard the occasional pheasant and the odd partridge as an understood thing, a sort of gentleman's agreement, a perquisite. And, anyway, if one is walking round the fields with a gun in a perfectly legitimate search for rabbits, and a pheasant gets up, or a covey of partridges—well, that is a temptation for the strongest will. Let those who, faced with it, have withstood it cast the first stone. There will not be many stones cast.

Where the rights have been let it is another matter. The tenant farmer, holding as he does a very low opinion of the letting of shooting rights, will succumb to temptation more frequently. And if in addition he feels really aggrieved about anything, or does not entertain any respect for the shooting tenant, then he seldom fails to take the law into his own hands, and to help himself as need and opportunity afford. And that is poaching. It is, moreover, poaching that is next door to impossible to stop. No matter how closely keepered the ground may be, the man who has a legitimate right to carry a gun enjoys endless opportunities of varying his bag, and uses them. Nor is the practice confined to small farmers or poor men—far from it; some of the big farmers are among the worst offenders. It will be a bold keeper who will take action against a farmer on his own ground: a bold keeper and a foolish one. I have known it done on two occasions. Each time the keeper, an honest and loyal, if not over-intelligent, servant to his master, suffered severely. He did not suffer personally—that is to say, he suffered no bodily harm. Every one was perfectly polite to him. But in each case there was a marked and rapid deterioration in the shooting.

It is not only the pheasant and the partridge—recognised game birds—that are taken in this way. Woodcock, snipe, and duck are regularly shot by farmers. Indeed, even those farmers who are scrupulous in their observance of the landlords' rights where pheasants and partridges are concerned—and it must not be thought, from what I have said, that their number is few—will shoot any woodcock they may happen to come across. It is not a bit of good talking about the right of " shooting and sporting ", whatever that may mean. It may have some effect where the landlord exercises the right to the shooting—at least so far as duck are concerned: I have never known it to be observed in the case of woodcock—it certainly has no effect where the rights have been let to a third party. Farmers, generally, regard the woodcock as their perquisite, no matter what shooting agreements there may be. And their argument is always the same: The woodcock is a bird of passage, and unless shot at sight may never be seen again. It is, therefore, foolish not to shoot it.

Actually, since woodcock and snipe are not game birds, a tenant farmer is perfectly within his rights in shooting them upon any ground that he occupies. But no woodcock and no snipe may legally be shot except by the holder of a game licence. (That does not apply to duck.) How many farmers are holders of game licences? A very small proportion, I'll be bound. But that does not prevent them shooting woodcock and snipe, pheasants and partridges. I have known farmers to boast that they have never

taken out a game licence. The ten-shilling is good enough. And
if they are caught and fined—a most unlikely contingency—they
will still be well in pocket. Somewhere I remember reading of a
farmer who boasted that he had saved £100 in the course of his
farming career, throughout which he had shot woodcock and snipe,
pheasants and partridges, by taking out only the ten-shilling
licence. That means that he had been shooting these birds for
forty years on a ten-shilling licence. If he was caught, then he
would at most be fined £5, so that he would still be £95 in pocket.
And that record must have been beaten many times. Why throw
good money away?

The fact is that the Game Laws over a great part of the country
are a dead letter. Close seasons are not observed by just those
men who should most observe them, and the game licence is ignored
by, I should guess, thousands who shoot annually. Pheasants are
shot in September, partridges in August, woodcock and snipe at
any time, by men with a ten-shilling licence. And the men who
would gladly see the Game Laws observed do not hesitate to break
the Wild Birds' Protection Acts. Neither the Game Laws nor the
Wild Birds' Protection Acts are, in fact, enforceable. They look
good enough on paper. They mean practically nothing.

It is against this background that one must consider the activities
of the ordinary poacher. It would be wrong to imagine that the
average poacher, even the average farm labourer who does a little
poaching, is ignorant of the law. So far as they are understandable,
the Game Laws are very well understood by the countryman. And
a great many farm labourers have a surprising knowledge of the
Wild Birds' Protection Acts. At least, they know both well
enough to know, or to guess, when they are being broken. And
though they break them themselves often enough, and break them
deliberately, they also know that they are being broken by those
who should know better—by their employers, by shooting men,
by gamekeepers, by men who will not, they know, be prosecuted,
as they themselves would be prosecuted if caught.

Chapter VIII

JUST POACHERS

"An' named? Well, last time that the beak—
Injustice, Sir, ain't far to seek;
I'd *found* the pheasants, so to speak,
   I'd got a rightful answer."

Patrick Chalmers.

EVERYONE who is familiar with the sporting Press will have noticed the insistence of those who write on shooting upon the need for keeping on the right side of the farmer and his labourers. That it is good policy to give an occasional rabbit to the labourers, especially around Christmas, is constantly rubbed in. And, of course, it is good policy. It does made a deal of difference. But why this insistence by writers on shooting matters? What does it really mean? It means that if the shooting tenant does not keep on the right side of the farmer and his labourers, there will be some falling off in the quality and quantity of the shooting, which is just another way of saying that there will be a lot of poaching, and that it will not be possible to stop it. And that is no more than the bare truth. There would be a lot of poaching, and it would not be possible to stop it.

The gamekeeper has not yet been born who could stop the poaching of game by farm labourers (and by farmers) if the latter were determined to poach. Gamekeepers are only human, and cannot be in more than one place at a time. Furthermore, the gamekeeper is not a fool—most of the gamekeepers I have known have been men of more than the average intelligence—and he knows well enough that his job can be made quite impossible by the men who work on the ground under his care if he gets on the wrong side of them. Most gamekeepers know—probably all of them know, but they will not all admit to the knowledge—that there is a great deal of what may be called "casual poaching" in the countryside, and they do nothing about it because they know they can do nothing about it. Only when it becomes more than casual, only when one man on the farm or farms takes more than the odd bird or rabbit—gets to making a routine practice of it and on an increasing scale—does the gamekeeper take action. And then he must know his man very well, and know his friends also. The gamekeeper should not be blamed for what may seem a dereliction of duty. He does his duty very well indeed. He does it better, indeed, than if he kept to the letter of his duty as it might be seen by his employer. If he did that, his employer would suffer badly. It should be remembered, too, that if the gamekeeper knows his ground and the habits and daily tasks of the men who work on it, those men, all of them, know him and his habits very much better still. They hold by right of inheritance the commanding position. So far as casual poaching is concerned, the gamekeeper has an impossible task.

And there is a great deal of casual poaching. I believe this is denied by many shooting men, and I know that a great many more just refuse to believe the evidence of their eyes. They like to think that the farm labourer is a model of rectitude so far as game is concerned. I should not like it to be thought that the farm labourer is a dishonest man. He is no more dishonest than the rest of us. There is, indeed, a much higher standard of honesty in the country than there is in the towns. One has only to think of the number of people living in the country who do not dream of locking their doors at night to realise the truth of that. The farm labourer has a very high standard of honesty. He works hard and he lives cleanly. He has a greater personal pride in his work than have men of the same standard of living in the towns. He is a craftsman and an individualist; he is no mere machine-minder. And he is a sportsman.

A sportsman and an individualist. Those characteristics are important. They are the characteristics upon which we, as a nation, pride ourselves most. We are, we say—and we say it loud and often—a nation of sportsmen. We are, we say—and we say it as often and usually a good deal louder—a nation of individualists: rugged individualists. Listen to talk in the Carlton Club and elsewhere where they have the interests of Empire at heart, and you will learn that it is just this rugged individualism of the British people that has made the British Empire what it is. And I would be the last to deny that. And as to sportsmanship: you can hardly open a paper, you can hardly pass a day, without reading or hearing something about our great sporting qualities as a nation. Particularly is that so in times of stress or crisis. And it is true, at least so far as the countryside is concerned. We are a nation of individualists and sportsmen. Yet, though we pride ourselves upon being a nation of sportsmen, we take care—or as much care as we can—that the practice of sport shall be confined to those with considerable financial resources. You cannot hunt without money; you cannot fish for salmon, and in many parts of the country for trout, without money; you cannot shoot without some money. The vast majority of the population—and that goes for the rural population also—simply cannot indulge in these amusements, no matter how much they may want to do so. They have not got the money. The pursuit of sport in Britain has to all intents and purposes become the close preserve of the wealthy and the well-to-do. Those who are neither, but of a certain social standing, can rely upon getting a fair amount of sport during the course of a year by means of invitation. Those who are neither, and of no social standing, can do without.

Now, that applies to the majority of country folk, who are just the folk in whom the sporting instinct is the strongest. But they do not do without. If they cannot get their sport within the law, they get it without. The national characteristics—individualism and love of sport—are there, and we must not be surprised if they manifest themselves occasionally. But we are surprised, and rather horrified. It is all part of that false philosophy that grew up with the Victorians and their exaggerated love of and respect for money. It goes no farther back than that. It is the philosophy that finds expression in such statements as " the battle of Waterloo was won on the playing-fields of Eton ". The battle was won on the village greens and the ploughed fields and in the back streets of Britain. It is the British people of every class, of every creed, religious and political, that have made Britain's greatness, and not the products of any one class or creed. It is just as false a philosophy to limit the sporting instinct to one class or to one financial stratum. But it has happened, and it will not be undone in the lifetime of any one now living. And it has made legally dishonest men of thousands of honest men.

I am quite sure that most of the casual poaching springs from a desire for sport—that desire which is considered so admirable in the well-to-do. It is most certainly not done for money, nor is it done, save in times of great depression, primarily for food. The results are eaten, of course, and the quarry is dictated by its tastiness—the uneatable is not poached. The labourer and his wife like the taste of pheasant, partridge, duck, rabbit, and hare just as much as their more financially blessed countrymen. Small blame to them. But it is the sporting instinct that is at the root of the matter, and not love of money or mere gluttony. And while I would not go so far as to say that every farm labourer poaches every now and again, I am quite sure that the sporting instinct is so strong that the vast majority do do so, and I should be astonished to find a single farm labourer who has not at some time in his career poached something.

Most of this poaching is truly casual—a rabbit knocked over in a hedgerow at opportunity, and that sort of thing. A little of it is done with nets and a dog and a ferret of a Sunday afternoon, but not as much as might be expected. And there is a good deal of setting of snares here and there to be visited on the way to and from work. None of it is clever, and it does very little harm. It is daylight stuff—the mere picking up of odds and ends. There is, of course, a certain amount of night poaching by farm labourers as well, though it never attains proportions that need cause concern, so long as the man remains a farm labourer.

But sometimes you find a man with bigger ideas. And usually these ideas are less pleasant and the man more cunning. In my experience such men have a grudge against the keeper to work off, and they cease to be concerned with the sport of catching something, and concentrate on doing the keeper harm. In one such case—the gamekeeper was a tactless fellow, but the grudge was a figment of the imagination, though, as is the way of such things, it grew and grew—the man took to robbing the nests of pheasants and partridges. But he was too cunning to take the eggs away as eggs. Like most farm labourers, he carried to work a can containing his tea. But in his case it contained milk only. Into this milk he would break the eggs, and, once home, he had all the

" With nets and a dog and a ferret of a Sunday afternoon."

ingredients for a really good custard, and a fine and healthy meal. That sort of thing is not easy to discover and stop.

I suppose that it is this sort of thing that has given rise to some of the stories about the cunning of poachers, and to the very considerable literature on the mentality of poachers. I must confess that I find this literature extraordinarily interesting, and extraordinary in its own right. So much of it is contradictory, so little of it bears any relation to the poacher as I know him. But it must be remembered that most of it appears in papers devoted to the interests of the gamekeeper, and most of the rest in works of fiction.

> One does not often hear of a poacher who is dumb, although a poacher is often struck dumb when suddenly dropped on by a keeper who he imagines miles distant, but that is only a temporary dumbness. He is soon again voluble. . . . If poachers were given a little less to talking about their exploits, the keeper would gain less of the knowledge which enables him to outwit them. . . . Beer has a wonderful effect in loosening tongues, and, knowing this, the poacher would be well advised to keep away from the ale-house and all its temptations to talk. One of his great faults is that he considers himself something of a hero because he defies the law, and to induce others to entertain the same opinion concerning him he is given to boasting of his deeds.

That is an extract from a sporting paper, an extract from an article entitled " The Mentality of the Poacher ". And here is an extract from another article in the same paper, an article entitled " Poachers' Mentality " :

> . . . Reading an article some time ago I received the impression that the writer as a general rule understood that poachers were strong in the arm and weak in the head. . . . I agree that in some cases the mentality of the poacher is not very high, but I think it will be found that the latter are not habitual poachers but men who make themselves a confounded nuisance to the keeper. . . . Speaking of the habitual poacher is a different matter altogether. He is often poaching under the keeper's nose when that worthy imagines him miles distant. The surprise is all the keeper's when he makes that lucky cop. . . . Ale loosens tongues, but unfortunately not only the poacher's. The next keeper who is having his coverts raided while he is having a drink or two won't be by any means the first.

Well, there you are—two articles from the same paper dealing with the same subject. They could not be more opposed. And both, it might be as well to point out, were written by gamekeepers.

The idea that poachers are drunkards and boasters is all too prevalent in the sporting world. The first of those two articles was, I am sure, the most popular with the readers of the paper. But the second is beyond doubt the most accurate. Listen again to the writer of the first article:

> Of one fact I am assured, this being that the average poacher is an unmitigated liar, inclined to gross exaggeration when relating his exploits; he would have you believe that game simply walks into his nets and snares, and that pheasants, like the American coon, come down from the trees rather than be shot at. If you accept what he says, the majority of gamekeepers ought to be consigned to lunatic asylums, so simple-minded are they, and so easily misled. The poacher never tries to explain why, if this state of affairs prevails, he has so often fallen into the keepers' clutches.

That accurately portrays the accepted view of the poacher—drunkard, boaster, and liar. And the writer goes on:

> No man ever succeeded in making a living by poaching, although he would have you believe that the result of one night's work provides him with sustenance for a fortnight or longer. The poacher's appearance reveals that he fares none too well, for he is usually ill-clothed, unkempt and shows all the signs of irregular living.

This is the picture of Sir Peter Jeffrey Mackie's poacher. It is what the landowner and the gamekeeper would like to believe. But it is far from the truth.

Against it put the picture drawn by the other writer to the same paper:

> I never got much information in a public-house. I have been in them, of course, but I never paid much attention to any man who boasted of his exploits, and I always watched the quiet, inoffensive person, the man who kept his own counsel and was civil to every one.

He has other sound words to deliver on the subject of public-houses also:

> I have found that most things have two meanings, whereby listeners, whether in public-houses, the gun-room, or on shooting day, are not always so friendly disposed to the keeper as that worthy imagines; and many a keeper's preserve has been raided

through his innocently letting slip something that would have been best kept to himself.

I know which of those two men I would employ as a gamekeeper. In a fairly extensive acquaintance with men who poach, and in a fairly extensive acquaintance with country ale-houses, I have never yet heard a man who does poach boast of his exploits. I have heard boasting, of course—quite a lot of it—but invariably it has come from men who do not poach, or so rarely and so amateurishly that it amounts to nothing. I do not think that I shall ever hear a good poacher boast. But I have heard, and shall hear again, boasting for a purpose. I have heard men tell the most unlikely stories, and a few that sound probable, in public-houses of an evening, and always there has been a gamekeeper present . . . and not infrequently there has been a raid going on at that very moment on that gamekeeper's preserves. Boasting is not always as innocent as it appears. But the real poacher is a silent man, as silent in his public-house as he is about his work. Poaching is a silent way of life.

And again, the description of the poacher as ill-clothed, unkempt and showing all the signs of irregular living, though it would strike a responsive chord in the breast of Sir Peter Jeffrey Mackie, is singularly inaccurate. The man whose appearance is such is altogether too noticeable, especially in the country, where normally there is not much irregular living. He would be the target for gossip by all the old dears of the village. They would know all about him and his habits, and they would invent for him additional and lurid pastimes, of which, of course, poaching would be one. In no time at all the police would know all about him as well, and so would all the gamekeepers. He would be a marked man, and a marked man cannot poach. The second writer is right in his estimate of the inmates of the public-house. He is right to suspect the quiet, inoffensive man who keeps his own counsel. And he is right in his estimation of the feelings of the customers of the village local towards the gamekeeper. It is not always as friendly as it appears on the surface. And this is natural. For the man as a man they may entertain the friendliest feelings. But he is also the representative, at second hand, of the law. He is, or he may be at any time, the enemy of someone in the village, and villagers are clannish. Gamekeepers as a whole are a remarkably fine body of men, but it would be idle to pretend that gamekeepers as a whole are a popular body of men in the countryside. And it is rare indeed that they get worth-while information about poachers in the village from the villagers; informers are not popular anywhere.

Writer No. 2 ends his article thus:

> I advise you all not to underrate the intelligence of some poachers. Remember force of circumstances kept them from lawfully participating in this sport. Remember the sporting instinct is strong. Some of our wealthiest business men are never so happy as when trailing round with a gun, stalking an old hare. We cannot wonder, then, that people not so lucky suffer seriously from the same urge. Nor is it always the common type of low intelligence that practise the pilfering of game. This has been proved time and again, especially now when cars are used, and the keeper must needs be of good intelligence to defeat this menace to his livelihood.

Writer No. 2 was, I think, a good gamekeeper. At least he did not swallow the usual guff, as did writer No. 1. But gamekeepers have changed a great deal of recent years, and I am doubtful if the teachings of Mackie would fall on such receptive ground now as they did when they were first published. I am not so sure that the landowners and the shooting tenants have altered as much, though. I find that the Mackie view of the poacher is still widely held by the shooting man.

It would be idle to pretend that all poachers are men of high or even good intelligence, as idle as it would be to pretend that all gamekeepers are good gamekeepers, that all gamekeepers are men of a high standard of intelligence. But just as the standard of intelligence among gamekeepers has improved enormously of recent years—and that is beyond question—so in all probability has the standard of intelligence among the poaching fraternity. Indeed, there has been an all-round improvement in the standard of intelligence of the nation, and it is most unlikely that poachers (since they come from all walks of life) have been deliberately excluded by the Almighty from sharing in this improvement. I can only say that my own experience of poachers has shown them to be men of very considerable intelligence, especially when it comes to a question of outwitting gamekeepers.

But it must not be supposed that I think that the poacher is a more intelligent man than the gamekeeper. Comparisons are always odious, and in this case they are also impossible. Most poaching goes unpunished. " Cops " are few and far between, and more often than not a matter of luck. The number of planned captures are few, probably very few, though one cannot expect a working gamekeeper to admit that they are. But this does not mean that the poacher is too clever for the gamekeeper. Between an expert gamekeeper and an expert poacher there is probably very little to choose in the matter of intelligence. But the dice are heavily weighted in favour of the poacher. The gamekeeper has a considerable area of land to guard and a considerable variety of game in his charge. The occasions on which he knows that a raid is to be made and where it is to be made and on what it is to be made are few indeed. The poacher can choose his spot from his knowledge of the keeper's habits, and he can choose his time, and he knows what it is he wants to capture. His knowledge of the countryside is at least as good as that of the keeper whose ground he raids, and he will, if he knows his job (and he is an expert, remember), have planned the raid down to the smallest detail long beforehand. Yes, the scales are heavily weighted in favour of the poacher.

But the fact that the scales are so heavily weighted in favour of the poacher does not mean that poachers are not clever. It is not all a matter of luck and long odds, as some would have us believe. Let us return to writer No. 1:

> I can assure readers that the poacher of romance does not exist; I have never yet met the merry freebooter represented by the pen of the fiction writer, the man so skilled in the life of field and wood that he does what he likes with God's creatures. The real poacher is far from being all that. We read so much about him and his dog, that marvellous animal capable of scenting a keeper half a mile away, who will meet his master at any given point, getting there by a different route to avoid raising suspicion. The dog is said, on seeing any one approaching, to slip through the roadside fence and obliterate itself till that person has passed out of sight. According to report, no hare can escape the poacher's dog : and if this is to be believed, I wonder it has not yet figured on the dog-tracks. The poacher feels that he must possess both gun and dog, but uses either very little, as they give his game away too palpably. Both are too noisy and too obvious.

I, too, have not yet met the poacher of romance nor the poacher beloved by the writer of sensational fiction. And I agree that no real expert at the art of poaching uses a gun. It is a noisy thing, and the essence of good and skilful poaching is silence. But writer No. 1, in his eagerness to show how mistaken we are on this subject of poaching and poachers, goes a little too far. He should know more about poachers' dogs than he does. And he should know that there are men who can do wonderful things " with God's creatures ". I know, for I have seen them.

Chapter IX

THE MOUCHER

Who doth ambition shun,
And loves to live i' the sun,
Seeking the food he eats,
And pleased with what he gets,
Come hither, come hither, come hither:
Here shall he see
No enemy
But winter and rough weather.

William Shakespeare.

MOUCHING, though you might not think so, is a profession. It is, moreover, a profession requiring a lengthy apprenticeship.

Billy Lovelock is a moucher. Lovelock is a Gypsy name, and there are Lovelocks in my neighbourhood, and others come in during the hop harvest. But Billy is not a Gypsy, though he may have a drop of the dark blood in his veins introduced far back in time. He is the son, the grandson, the great-grandson of labourers who have all worked on the same farm. I do not know when Billy left regular farm work and started on his own, but he has been a moucher to my certain knowledge for twenty years and more. He is now well over seventy, but you could not tell his age by looking at him. His face is like an old walnut, his hair is grey (it would be white if he had a shampoo), and rather too long and wispy. He is a gaunt man and bent. But his eyes—small and round and jet black, like the ends of the hat-pins my nurse used to

wear—are as alert and wicked as those of young jackdaws. And
he is only deaf when he does not want to hear. Gaunt and bent
and thirty years older than I am he may be, yet I find it difficult to
keep up with him when we spend a day together in the country.

Billy lives in a cottage tucked into the shoulder of the down
about two miles from the village, a cottage that is a good deal more
lonely than its distance from other habitations would suggest. It
was derelict when Billy took it over after the first German War.
The two bedrooms stood open to the sky, the roof was no more
than a rafter or two. Grasses, mosses, ivy grew in the walls. The
windows were broken or glassless, and most of the floorboards
were missing. Going upstairs was an adventure. I remember
the cottage in this state well, for it was empty and more or less
derelict when I was a child. It was reputed to be haunted (all
empty buildings in this part of the world are haunted: it is the
tradition), and it became one of my great adventures to enter it
and to climb the rickety, half-absent staircase and scare the bats
from the corners of the bedroom. A family of feral cats lived in
one of the rooms downstairs, and on one of my visits scared the
wits out of me. Another time, when I was about half-way up the
stairs, a great bird—an owl it must have been, but childish imagination (I was then about ten) made it an eagle—crashed past my
head and out through a hole in the wall that was once a window.
Derelict, indeed, was that cottage; the home of many animals and
birds, and innumerable insects, and armies of spiders. It had not
served as home for human for nearly twenty years when Billy, to
the astonishment of the whole village, took it and its wilderness of
a garden over for a purely nominal rent. He did the necessary
repairs (which meant, in fact, a rebuilding job) himself with such
materials as he could lay hands on. He is not the sort of man to
buy anything if he can pick up something that can be made to serve
the purpose for nothing. He bought nothing for this cottage, as
he told me himself—and I believe he spoke truth—save only glass
for the windows. As a result, the building, and especially the roof
as you look down upon it from the hill-top, appears a little odd.
But at least it is water-tight, and that is what matters most in a
house.

While this was going on Billy and his wife camped in one of the
rooms downstairs, rigging up an old tarpaulin to serve as roof.
Both worked on the house, and while Billy was away in search of

suitable building material his wife attacked the wilderness that was meant to be a garden. Mrs. Billy is a foreigner. She hails from Portsmouth, and came to this neighbourhood as a domestic servant. Any one who comes to our village from such distant parts as Portsmouth, though that is in the same county, is a foreigner, but Mrs. Billy has true foreign blood in her veins also. Her father, she says, was a wandering Breton onion-seller, which is very probable. There is a good deal of Breton blood along the south coast of England. She acquired Billy for husband by the usual country method of those days—and perhaps the method has not changed so much—of trial and error, and in her case a miscarriage. She is an enormous mountain of fat, a huge, rolling, cheerful slattern as strong as an ox. And she is a very good wife to a very difficult man. She attacked the wilderness with terrific energy, sweating and swearing all the time, and losing no weight at all. Then, when her husband returned pushing his laden barrow before him, she would leave the garden and help him with whatever the job might be on the house, leaving him only to cook a meal. More than once in those days I shared a meal with the Lovelocks, and good meals they were, though I was always careful not to inquire too closely how the contents of the pot were acquired. All this work on the derelict building and the surrounding jungle took time. Indeed, it must have taken years to get the place into good condition, and long before that happened Billy had bought the cottage and the land that went with it. It was cheap enough, I warrant, but where the money came from I do not know. Probably Billy, like so many countrymen, who do not appear as though they had two pennies to rub together, had more than a little put by. Probably he had been saving with this cottage in view for many years. Years slip by in the country, and their passage is not noticed. I do not know how long it took before Billy brought his furniture from the barn where it had been stored, borrowing a horse and cart from the farmer for the purpose. I do not know how long it took to turn the jungle into a garden. I am sure that no one, including Billy and his wife, has any idea. But now the garden is as good an example of a cottage garden as you will find for many miles around. And if you were to go into the cottage you would find it difficult indeed to believe that it had once been a roofless, windowless wreck, and that it had been brought to its present state solely by the efforts of these two old people, by their hands alone, and with materials scrounged here and there in the neighbourhood.

There are some surprises inside that cottage, too. There is a very nice old Welsh dresser. There is a grandfather clock made in Devizes (where once there was a famous clockmaker); but that should not be a surprise—some of the nicest grandfather clocks I have seen have been in farm-labourers' cottages. There is a round table that would make most antique dealers green with envy. And there is some really good old china. (In this respect many farm labourers are like Gypsies: they do not have much china, but what they do have is good and old—Staffordshire and the like. They have no room for the modern and cheap production.) The few pictures are abominable, but the china is above reproach. Old china is Billy's passion. He really loves it. Once I lent him a book about it, which he read with great difficulty, since his education had ceased at the age of ten or thereabouts, and was in any case only the village education of the period. But he did read it, and I found out later that he had, with enormous labour, copied out the illustrations of it into an old penny notebook—the marks of the old makers. This impressed me so much that I bought him a copy of the book. Now, I should guess, he knows all the marks and most of the designs; but beyond that he has a real feeling for china, an instinct for the good, a flair for picking up good pieces— a flair born of love. He discovered one day during a fleeting visit to my house that I had an old Staffordshire sheep, a singularly ugly sheep with a singularly foolish expression on its face, but a very early example of genuine Staffordshire work. I told him nothing about it, but merely watched him handling it, which he did for quite a while, caressing it with his large, brown, hairy hands before giving it back to me, without a word. A year or two ago (which was some five years after I had shown him that sheep) I wanted a large privet hedge cut. Labour, since it was war-time, was in very short supply, and I could get no one to do it. One day Billy appeared, and informed me that he would cut my hedge for me. I asked him what the job would cost. He wanted no money. He wanted the sheep and his meals. We struck the bargain. The job took him two full days, eight-thirty to five or so, and he did it really well. At the end he would take no money. But he had the sheep, and was obviously delighted with his bargain. I have often wondered if his wife was as delighted. But Billy makes some money out of china, for he is a dab hand at repairing chipped or broken pieces, and is in demand with the village women for miles around for this purpose. Mostly the gentry and the well-to-do generally will not use his skill, for they do not regard him as a man to be " encouraged ".

In the country the classes are much more clearly defined than in the towns. In particular, there is still a very sharp division between the leisured and the working classes. For a man of the working class to have no regular job, to have no employer, to have no clear and easily recognisable means of support, is in the eyes of the leisured class a sin of the first magnitude. In the towns the classes merge into each other, and there is in any case a very large number of people without regular jobs—without jobs at all for that matter—and always there are people of apparent affluence without visible means of support. Towns are busy places, and no one has the time or the inclination to bother about such people or what they do to live. Not so in the country. Here a man without a regular job, if he be of the working class, is an object for suspicion to the leisured classes, and all sorts of dark deeds, roughly covered by the word poaching, are laid at his door. Especially is this so in a neighbourhood such as my own, where the leisured class is composed almost entirely of retired Service people, with strong feelings on the subject of work and discipline, and usually almost as strong feelings on the subject of sport. Here a man such as Billy is regarded as a good-for-nothing, idle fellow, and one definitely not to be " encouraged "—except perhaps when another beater is required—for Billy is a moucher.

Now, mouchers may be all sorts of things, but they are most certainly not idlers. On the contrary, a moucher is a most industrious person (he must be, if he is not to starve), though his code of ethics—like that of the successful business man—is peculiarly his own. Mouching is a profession. It requires a very long apprenticeship, and it involves very hard work once that apprenticeship has been served, which is why you do not as a rule find more than one moucher in a district (and a large district at that). All mouchers seem to be old men. At any rate I have never come across a young moucher. As I have said, Billy is now well over seventy, and though I do not know for certain when he left regular farm work and took to mouching, it was not much more than twenty years ago. In other words, Billy did not adopt the profes-

sion until he was fifty. And I do not think that any moucher
becomes a moucher until he is fifty or thereabouts, for a younger
man would scarcely have had sufficient time in which to acquire the
knowledge that is necessary. Mouching requires a longer apprenticeship than any other profession in the world. It begins as
soon as schooldays are over (in times past that was at twelve years
old or even younger), though in exceptional cases—if, for example,
the lad is big physically—it may begin during school days, and it
continues all the while the man is working as a labourer, and up
to the age of fifty or so. But this long apprenticeship is not in
itself sufficient, no matter how brilliant the pupil may be. There
are, in addition, certain well-defined characteristics that are essential.
A great many countrymen of fifty and over have the necessary
knowledge to become mouchers. Not many have the necessary
character.

Apprenticeship—in my neighbourhood, at least—begins on a
Sunday. On Sundays the lads of the village go for a walk. They
do not go singly or in pairs. They do not go with girls. They
go all together, a dozen or so together. This does not mean that
they have not got girls; far from it. Almost certainly they have,
for most country boys have a girl shortly after leaving school, if
not before. But girls have nothing to do with this walk. There
are six evenings in the week a boy can waste on girls if he has a
mind to do so. On Sunday afternoons every right-minded boy
walks. It is the custom. A boy joins the walk when he leaves
school, just as his father and his grandfather, just as the village men
for generations had done. And when a youth leaves the walk to
walk with a girl, everybody in the neighbourhood knows what it
means. It means, ninety-nine times out of a hundred, that the girl
is pregnant. It is as good as putting up the banns.

So on Sundays you would come across the boys walking. They
would be drifting aimlessly along the lanes, hands in trousers'
pockets, and they would be pretty well straggled out, and most
of the time they would be silent. Occasionally you would come
across a party kicking a tennis-ball along, but usually they would
be just lounging along. It certainly looked very dull and aimless.
And I have often heard the gentry, and especially the older and
blimpier gentry, say things about decadence and when they were
boys. But, then, they were not the sons of farm labourers. And
it could not have been dull, for the boys would not have done it

H

if it had been. Country boys are no more fond of dullness than town boys, have just as rooted an objection to boredom. And if those blimpier gentry had looked a little more closely at the walk, they might have begun to wonder a bit.

For one thing, one or two of the boys would be carrying sticks, and one or two of the boys would have dogs. And the dogs—they would always be the quiet sort—would not be walking in the road. Closer examination would have shown that the walk is by no means as aimless as it appears, that there is a good deal of method about it.

The Sunday walk is, in fact, the village university. At school the boys get a bit of " learning ". In the walk they learn the things that will really be useful to them in after-life—the lie of the land, the way of birds and beasts, the little hidden places where good things grow in profusion.

That sort of knowledge, it may be thought, could only be of value to ne'er-do-wells. Nothing could be farther from the truth. That sort of knowledge is, of course, particularly valuable to the ne'er-do-well, but it is also of immense value to all countrymen working on and living by the land, men who will in all probability live most of their lives in the one neighbourhood, will marry and raise families (probably large families), and who will never have more than a pound or two in a week. Farm-labourers' wages have risen as a result of war, but so has the cost of living. Farm-labourers' wages before the war were terribly small, and they are likely to shrink again as soon as the competition for exports gets back into its stride. Low wages did not matter so much in the pre-enclosure days. But the enclosures took much from the peasant that was his by ancient right, and the small wages paid instead did not compensate him for the loss. The walk, I think, dates from the enclosures. Time was when the farm labourers earned no more than eight to twelve shillings a week, and, though living was cheap then, the money was not sufficient to provide adequately for a large family. It was not intended to be. A large, landless, pauperised peasantry was part—an essential part—of the wealth of Britain. From it were drawn the workers that made possible the Industrial Revolution. Rises in wages came, of course, but each rise was accompanied or, more usually, preceded by a yet steeper rise in the cost of living. Probably the farm labourer has never been so poor as when he was earning, in the twenties and thirties of this century, some thirty shillings or less in a week : in the days when our bacon came from Denmark, our butter from Denmark and New Zealand, our mutton from New Zealand and Australia, most of our beef from Argentina, our eggs from Denmark, Portugal and even, *mirabile dictu*, China; in the days when our countryside, bankrupted in the interest of our foreign investments (cloaked by the parrot-cry of cheap food), was degenerating into a game preserve for the city magnate. The need for the walk was even greater in the 'twenties and 'thirties than it had been in the immediate post-enclosure period. The farm labourer has no foreign investments.

A really intimate knowledge of the countryside is essential to success as a moucher. Most countrymen—most farm labourers, at any rate—have a sound working knowledge of their immediate neighbourhood, knowledge acquired on the walk, and increased through the years by the very nature of their daily tasks, but comparatively few have a really intimate knowledge. Among the better-to-do of the rural population, by the way, any real knowledge of the countryside in which they live is conspicuous by its absence. Some of the women know where to find certain flowers, some of the women have some idea, though usually a very vague idea, of the whereabouts of the commoner wild fruits. But scarcely any of the men have any real knowledge of the countryside in which they live. Even though they may own the land and live on it throughout the year, even though they may ride over it constantly, shoot over it regularly, fish its streams, they never acquire more than a working knowledge of its salient features. How many owners or tenants of shootings know where the birds they hope to shoot nest? How many owners or tenants of shootings could lead a visitor to all the partridge nests on their ground? They do not have to know: they employ gamekeepers. But the farm labourer, if he is to stock his larder free of charge as often as possible, must know a good deal about the countryside. And the moucher, who is going to earn the whole of his living off the countryside, and who almost invariably has no other source of income, must know it intimately—really intimately.

Let us consider a few of the means by which a moucher earns his livelihood.

His year may be said to begin in February (incidentally, the only year that begins on January 1st seems to be the calendar year), when he collects moss, sackfuls of it. The florists buy it for wreaths and such-like, and the moucher will, maybe, earn eight shillings or so in a day this way. It sounds easy enough, collecting moss and selling it to florists. But all moss will not do. The moucher must get the right sort, and he may have to walk ten miles in the day to get it. That means not only that he must know the right sort, but also where the right sort grows, and that means that he must know the short-cuts to these places. For if he does not, he will have to walk much more than ten miles in the day, or earn less than his eight shillings. He must, in fact, know his countryside very well indeed.

Then at the end of March and early in April there are flowers—primroses and sweet violets and daffodils. Here he meets competition—not from other mouchers, but from Gypsies and from ordinary citizens, and, especially where primroses and sweet violets are concerned, from children. But the flower business is a profitable one. Twopence a bunch used to be the price asked for primroses and sweet violets, and decked out in a big basket they sold readily, and so did cowslips. The price has gone up now. Sixpence a bunch is often asked and received now. But they sell just as well, and they do not take any more trouble to pick. But to make good money out of flowers the moucher must know not only where they grow in sufficient quantities to be worth picking, but also just when they will be coming into bloom, for if he arrives a day late he will find nothing much to pick, and will have had a walk, perhaps a long walk, for nothing. Even more forcibly does this apply to daffodils, for daffies (by the way, *daffs* in polite society, *daffies* to everybody else) are eagerly sought after by Gypsies. Daffodils do grow wild in profusion in certain places, and if there is such a place in the neighbourhood, the moucher will be sure to know of it, and will do his best to forestall the Gypsies. But the best daffs grow in private gardens—which is a great temptation to the honest moucher. Daffies fetch more than primroses or sweet violets, and are therefore worth seeking diligently—even at the cost of conscience. And daffodil bulbs may be transplanted easily—a point known to every moucher worth his salt. Billy's daffies are superb.

Then there is watercress. Watercress is picked twice a year—spring and autumn—and most mouchers farm their own watercress, planting it themselves and tending it carefully. If you do not know the ways of mouchers, this will probably surprise you. Watercress farms imply a certain amount of capital and a certain amount of labour. But a moucher does not have to own land to farm

". . . early in April there are . . . primroses."

watercress. All he requires is a brook—a nice quiet brook away from the hub of things. There are plenty such in England, and quite a few in my neighbourhood. Lovelock makes a very good thing out of his watercress, selling it from door to door in the towns (" nice fresh watercress "; the freshness assured by a wet sack to keep out the rays of the sun). Occasionally he sells in considerable quantities to a shop, but the door-to-door trade is the more profitable: good money earned with very little trouble and the help of somebody else's water.

There is good money to be made out of ferns also. It is harder work, this. Harder, because the moucher must sell his ferns from door to door in the better-class streets of the towns, and this means that he must get himself known and accepted as a seller of good plants of all sorts. This sometimes takes a very long time, and living is poor until acceptance comes, but, once accepted as a seller of good plants of all sorts, from ferns to primroses, from daffodils to blackberries, living is good. It is harder also because a whole day will have to be spent in digging up the roots and packing them to carry home, a whole day and a long walk. But fern roots sell at anything from threepence to sixpence, according to the mental hardness of the housewife (there are few better judges of female character than a moucher), and a day's digging should bring in a pound, or even more. Again the moucher must know not only where ferns grow in profusion, but also something about ferns. You do not sell a dud twice.

From the end of May until well into July honeysuckle is a great stand-by. There are several sorts of honeysuckle, but they are all good sellers at anything from sixpence to a shilling a bunch. Honeysuckle grows wild, but not in any great quantity, and not infrequently it grows best in private gardens. No matter where it grows, the moucher must know, and know, too, when it will flower. Billy once had the good fortune to discover that the tenants of a house with two particularly fine plants had gone to Bournemouth for a holiday just at flowering time, which saved him a long walk by night.

After haysel there are button mushrooms to be had for the gathering, and there is also centaury. There is a strong demand from herbalists for centaury. Dried, it is used as a tea by Gypsies and many country people—and a very good drink it is, too—and it is also thought to be good for consumption. It has other pro-

perties as well—in Hampshire it is called by the country people
" Christ's Ladder," which is a contraction of " Christ's Ladder to
Heaven "—and in the hands of a moucher with a smooth tongue
and a smattering of herbal lore it is a certain money-maker, not
only among country people, but also in the towns, and in the
good-class houses at that.

With autumn comes the real mushroom. A good moucher
reckons to make quite a lot of money in the autumn out of mushrooms and blackberries. Mushrooms entail very early rising—
there is competition here also—and a very sound knowledge of
the ground, but the money makes any trouble worth while. Mushrooms grow in all sorts of places. But no man who is going to
make money by gathering and selling them is going to waste time
on any but the best places. It is said—and earnestly believed by
most countrymen and all mouchers—that really good mushrooms
will grow only where there has been a stallion, and that in any case
fields that have not held horses regularly are not worth searching.
I do not know what foundation there is for that bit of country lore
(it will be greeted with contempt by all the expert mushroom-
growers), but I do know that Billy Lovelock finds more and better
mushrooms than any one else in the neighbourhood, and that he
believes it implicitly. There is no difficulty in selling mushrooms.
Generally they are sold to shopkeepers—probably to one shopkeeper only in a town—and no shopkeeper in his senses will haggle
overmuch with a moucher about the price. He knows full well
that if he does he will next year get no offer of mushrooms, and he
knows, too, that the moucher can always get a good and regular
door-to-door trade in the good-class districts, and that some of
that trade will come from himself. To prevent this he will pay
the moucher's price, and the moucher, in order to avoid several
long walks, will be reasonable in his charges.

Just as the moucher knows where the best mushrooms grow, so
he will know where the best blackberries grow. The quantities
that an energetic moucher will pick in a day are prodigious—
twenty and thirty pounds at a time. Remember your own blackberrying expeditions, and the time you spent, and the quantity you
picked, and how disappointingly little they weighed when you got
them home, and you will have some idea of the labour picking
thirty pounds must entail. To see Billy Lovelock returning from
a blackberrying expedition is enough to make one give up black-

berrying for all time. But, then, he knows the countryside, which
most blackberry-pickers do not. There is money in blackberries
as there is in mushrooms, and so the best places are known and, so
far as possible, kept secret. Farmers, too, know that there is
money in them, and so occasionally (more frequently nowadays
than a few years ago) you will see notices put up announcing that
these blackberries or mushrooms are "cultivated". They are
not, of course; they are as wild as nature intended them to be. I
do not know what effect such notices have on townsfolk out for
the day—very little, I expect. But I do know that they have no
effect at all on country people. They are against all tradition.

Though, naturally, the means by which a moucher earns his
living vary from district to district—a fell-land moucher will
obviously have different sources of income from a moucher of the
flat lands of Lincolnshire or a moucher of the Sussex Weald—the
essential for success in all mouching remains the same: a truly
intimate knowledge of the countryside. I have outlined above
what I believe to be the staple sources of income of one Hampshire
moucher. Probably they do not differ very much for mouchers
all over the southern downland. To these must be added, of course,
many side-lines, things which do not occur regularly, or even
frequently, but which are turned to good account whenever opportunity offers. These side-lines will vary from man to man,
according to personal taste and ability as well as opportunity.
Lovelock, for example, sometimes makes money out of bulrushes
and sometimes out of heather. Good, long-established tailors are
fond of decorating their windows with bulrushes (the custom unfortunately seems to be dying out), and Lovelock on his visits to
town keeps an eye on the windows of the one firm that still holds
fast to the tradition. The highest-class game-dealers like to
arrange heather with their grouse and partridges. Lovelock will
supply their need. There are many such side-lines—holly and
greenery for Christmas decoration are other examples. And there
are others. Almost all mouchers—I would be safe, I think, in
saying all mouchers—have been farm labourers for many years
before they became mouchers. Farm labourers are like sailors—
exceptionally handy men. So Lovelock will sharpen a saw, mend
old china, grind a lawn-mower, do a hundred and one jobs—provided that he likes the person who wants the job done, and provided
that it is not a long job. Only exceptionally—as, for example, for

a Staffordshire china sheep which he wanted badly—will he under-take anything that is likely to interfere with his freedom of move-ment, his independence, for more than an hour or so. It is this intense independence of character that makes a man take to mouch-ing. Mouchers are men who will call no man master.

In addition to the many side-lines, that vary from man to man according to personal inclination, there is one side-line that is com-mon to all mouchers everywhere—the taking of a rabbit here, a hare there, a bird as occasion offers. A snare or two are light enough, and take up little or no room, and a man who is abroad in the fields and hedgerows the day through soon learns where to set them. There is nothing wholesale about it. The moucher does not poach to sell. He poaches to eat. He is concerned neither with money nor sport. He is concerned only with his own larder, and the need to keep it supplied. He likes to have game to eat: he has always had game to eat. But he would be furious if he was called a poacher. A poacher is one who steals to sell, a thief.

Billy Lovelock uses snares only. He has a dog, but it does not accompany him on his outings. It is an old and lazy half-spaniel, and is company for the old woman. He has no gun. What would he need a gun for? A stone is a good weapon—a good and dangerous weapon in the hands of a man who can throw. I have seen a rabbit killed as clean as a whistle by a well-aimed stone, and Billy Lovelock has killed more than one hare in its form by means of a well-aimed stone. But you must know your stone. And since the right sort of stone is not so easy to find, it is advisable to retrieve it after it has been thrown. But the snare is safer. Two or three well-set snares a day will keep the wolf from the door, and for a man going a long walk in the byways, and knowing the habits of the keepers, there is little chance of being caught. I think that I am right in saying that in all his life Billy Lovelock has never been caught by the gamekeepers with game in his possession. That is the reward of skill.

To be a successful moucher you must know the country very well indeed. You learn to know it by walking on Sunday after-noons . . . a dozen or so together.

Chapter X

DOGS

I know you love me, and I hope you honour;
I want to be as sure about *obey*;
E'en when temptations fall most thick upon her
No lady should, I think, break clean away;
Her youth may trifle with some fancy gay,
But prompt she heeds, be she of good repute,
Her lord's " Come in, you brute! "

Patrick Chalmers.

THE dog is an essential part of sport in Britain. We could not hunt without it, we could not shoot without it, and there are those who maintain that you cannot poach without it. There is an enormous literature centred around hounds. But it is a specialised literature, and deals but little with the hound as a dog, as a personality. It is more concerned with him or her as a part of a science. Almost the reverse is true of the shooting dog. There is also a huge literature centred around him, but he has managed to keep himself clear of the science of shooting; he has managed to keep his personality inviolate. The huntsman never regards, cannot regard, the hound as a companion. The shooting man always regards the shooting dog as a companion.

Host, keeper, companions, may make or mar the fortunes of the day; but one's dog is always a distinct addition to one's pleasure— if not always to that of one's neighbour. He is a real companion, he rejoices in our kills—though I am not sure that he does not prefer a runner—he sympathises in our misses. The whole time he is taking the keenest interest in the sport. His wistful, appealing, upward glance, when he wants to tear off to retrieve a bird; his proud pleasure when, allowed to go, he returns in triumph with the bird; his conscious knowledge of his crimes, when sore and sudden temptation masters him, and his delight when the licking is over. All this is charming and for this and many other traits one loves him wisely, if too well.

So Earl Buxton in *Fishing and Shooting*. And he has accurately summed up the feelings of ninety-nine out of every hundred shooting men.

Indeed, shooting men take the greatest pride in the accomplishments of their dogs—often a greater pride than the accomplishments of the animal warrant. If the love of a man for a woman is blind, it is far-sighted indeed compared to the love of a shooting man for his dog. Too often, especially in advertisements, is the confirmed runner-in described as " steady as a rock ". Too often does the well-trained retriever of the bar-parlour turn out to be as wild as a kitten in the field. Yet the failing is one of the better traits of the human nature. Much of the best of a man goes into his love for a dog.

There was a time, of course, when the dog was of greater importance in the field than it is now. But conditions, though they have changed greatly since the days of St. John, have not changed so greatly that we can get through a day's shooting without a dog to aid us. Yet, though the average shooting man relies so much on his dog and takes so great a pride in its accomplishments, not one in a dozen shooting men takes any very great trouble or interest in the training of his dog. Too often they just get a dog at the beginning of the season from some dealer, quite regardless of its appearance or its qualifications. All shooting men, fortunately, are not like that. There are many who are interested in the possession of a really accomplished dog, but even of these there are few indeed who take any active interest in the actual training of the dog. They leave that to the keeper. And taking the country as a whole, the amount of attention paid by gamekeepers to the training of gun-dogs is not what it should be, though there has been a considerable improvement of recent years. A good keeper should be able to train a dog for the moor or the covert as well as be able to rear pheasants and to trap vermin. It is a part of the duty of a good keeper. But how many of them know anything about it?

Compare the average keeper's dog with the average shepherd's dog. There can be no question as to which is the most intelligent and which is the most useful to its master. Most shooting men would disagree violently with the suggestion that the collie is naturally more intelligent than the retriever, the pointer or the spaniel. If this attitude is the right one, then it must be a matter of training, and the average gamekeeper would maintain that he had not the time to devote to the business that the shepherd has, which is not true, for the gamekeeper has plenty of odd times that could be made use of in the training of his dogs and which are not in fact so utilised.   Leaving aside the question of intelligence for the moment, let us consider the question of training.   It is not very difficult to see why the average collie is so much better than the average gun-dog.   He is given more work, but he is given it so gradually that his brain is able to absorb and remember his lessons. And he is given work *daily*: he is made to do *the same things daily*.   What happens to the average gun-dog?   He is taken out on a string perhaps a dozen times (usually not as often as that) in a year, and expected to do a dozen different things each time.   He is never given a chance to learn the rudiments of his job.   No shepherd would make that elementary error.   And so it is that when we see a really well-trained gun-dog we marvel.   He stands out head and shoulders above his fellows.   There are about half a dozen expert gun-dog trainers in this country—no more.   There are perhaps three who stand out even among this half-dozen.   I believe I could tell dogs trained by them no matter where I was to see them and no matter under what conditions.

The gun-dog, however, labours under another handicap which does not affect the collie.   This is the canine exhibition.   The canine exhibition has done a lot of good, of course.   Of that there can be no doubt.   But it has also done an immense amount of harm.   Of that also there can be no doubt.   That the sporting dog has suffered less than most of the breeds is beyond question, always excepting the spaniel.   The bull-terrier has been ruined— look at the bull-terriers of the Potteries and you will realise that the bull-terrier of the south is a shadow of what the breed should be. The fox-terrier is in a like plight.   And the " fanciers " have played havoc with the spaniels.   The average spaniel to be seen at a canine exhibition is a grotesque creature with little or no brain, and so poorly formed that it is only with difficulty that it can get round the ring two or three times, and so catch the judges' eyes. The good sporting spaniel would stand no chance whatever of getting an award at any canine exhibition in the land.   Its head would be too broad, its ears too short, its legs too strong, and so on.   We have developed two breeds, or rather types, of spaniel in this country.   Unfortunately, the non-utility is much more popular than the utility, and bids fair to extinguish it within a measurable space of time.

As some counter to the attractions of the Show Bench there are the field trials. Field trials date back in this country to 1875, when the Kennel Club held its first Field Trial Derby at Orwell Park. Now there are many field trials, local and national. There are pointer and setter trials, retriever trials, and spaniel trials. Interest in these varies. There has been a marked falling off in the public interest in pointer and setter trials, for example, and the reason is not far to seek. Nowadays the sportsman prefers his game driven to him. Shooting over dogs is no longer as fashionable as once it was. Changed conditions in farming practice have had something to do with this—short-stubble fields have done away with the necessity for pointers and setters for partridge-shooting—but in the main it is the speed of modern life that has done the damage. We want our bags quickly nowadays. We want them too quickly for the use of pointers and setters. Even in Scotland, where there are still areas where grouse lie well, and where pointers and setters could be used with advantage, the tenant is usually in a hurry and wants to get south again by September.

Pointer and setter trials are for the most part held in the early spring, when the birds have paired, but before they have begun to nest, and when the cornfields are just high enough to provide some decent cover for the birds. If they are not held then, they are held just before the shooting season opens. The disadvantage of these late trials is that the game is not actually shot and killed, though a blank shot is fired to test for steadiness, and so there is not the temptation to run in on a falling bird. I am not at all sure of the value of these pointer and setter trials. The tests given are good so far as steadiness and game-finding are concerned, but I am doubtful if they provide a real test for stamina. Each dog does not have sufficient trial for this to be discovered, and I have often wondered how some of the best and fastest and most brilliant winners I have seen would fare during a long day after grouse in rough heather. Not very well, I fancy.

Retriever trials are held over one or two or three days, according to the size of the stake. In the big stakes three judges are appointed. One takes the right side of the line, one the centre, and one the left, and each has two guns to shoot for him. Each judge calls for the dogs he wishes independently of the other judges. Retriever trials have become very popular, and are as fair as they can be made, but even so there are seldom trials held that do not cause a lot of high feeling among the owners of unsuccessful dogs, and there are always accusations of favouritism that are quite uncalled for. I suppose that most of this ill-feeling arises from dogs being put out for hard mouth. But the rule that no dog shall be put out for hard mouth unless all three judges have examined the game puts any question of favouritism out of the realms of possibility, and makes the possibility of any mistake on the point very small indeed—provided always that the judge knows where and how the dog got the bird. This is most important. It is a simple enough question if the bird was dead in roots or in the open; it is a simple enough question if the bird was a runner in roots or in the open. Then if it is crushed or severely pinched, the answer is obvious. But if it is a dead bird that has fallen into a thick thorn-bush or fence; if it is a runner that has got into a thick thorn-bush, or under cut wood, or partly into a rabbit-hole, then the matter is not so simple, for the dog must use force to extract it. A good judge must know the conditions. Any judge can deal with such faults as running in. That is a fatal error easily dealt with so far as that particular stake is concerned. But it is not so easy a matter to judge just how much force is necessary to retrieve a bird. Taking the trials over the country as a whole, it may safely be said that the dogs which score are the dogs which show the most brains. This is another way of saying that the dogs that win under the judges are the dogs which are the most adaptable, the dogs which change their methods to suit the conditions.

Spaniel trials differ a good deal from retriever trials. There are, for example, two judges and a referee. One judge takes the right of the line, and the other takes the left, and each usually has two guns to shoot for him. That is for single-dog stakes. For brace or team stakes both judges work together and watch the work done. Up to about 1914 it was common to see several teams entered for trials. Nowadays one scarcely ever sees a team, and I think that is a great pity, for the teams were very popular with spectators.

Successful spaniel trials depend on the suitability of the ground, and on the amount of rabbits available and in the right place. Too many rabbits are the reverse of helpful, and bare ground is the reverse of helpful also. Too many rabbits make good work impossible, for they foil the ground as they move away ahead of the line. Bare ground makes good work impossible, as rabbits will not lie out, especially if the weather is bad. Further than this, the ground must be such as to enable the judges to see what the dogs are doing. Thus, ground with wood, furze or broom of any height is no good, since on such ground it is quite impossible to see what the dogs are actually doing. I think that the ideal ground is either open rough grass with clumps of thick brambles or open woodland with bracken and bramble clumps or heather and rushes. As with retrievers, the dogs that win under the judges are the dogs that use their brains, the dogs that are the most adaptable and change their methods to suit the conditions.

The dogs that are entered for field trials are, of course, trained animals, though from the amount of running in he sees the spectator might be forgiven for disbelieving that. Only a small proportion of the shooting dogs of the country are entered for field trials. What about the average shooting dog, the dog that will never see a field trial? I think that it may safely be said that the average shooting dog is badly trained or untrained, a perfect example of good material gone to waste. And this is true up to a point even of those dogs trained by professionals. But do not blame the professionals. They have done their job well enough—perfectly in the case of some half-dozen—but the trained dog is no longer in their charge. Blame the owners. The dog may be perfectly trained in the kennels of some professional, and while in that kennel will act as a perfectly trained gun-dog should act. It is what happens when he reaches his home from the kennels that matters. It is beyond doubt that the vast majority of shooting men who spend a good deal of money in having their dogs trained have no idea how to handle them when they return from the kennels. I suppose that the most important days in the life of a gun-dog are the few days immediately following his departure from the training kennels. It takes months to train a gun-dog properly; the whole of that training can be undone in an hour. Yet very few men trouble to go to the kennels to see their dog or dogs being trained and handled before they take them over. Dogs are individuals: each has its own characteristics; yet very few owners trouble to ask the trainer if their dog has any idiosyncrasies and what they are. They just go and take him over. They may remember to ask for a few words of command—they probably will forget even that important point—but that is all. And then they wonder why their dog, on which they have spent such a lot of money, is no better than the next-door dog on which no money has been spent in the matter of training, and the poor trainer gets the blame and suffers in reputation also. It is not really any wonder that the average shooting dog compares unfavourably with the average collie.

Intelligence does play a part, of course, and a big part, too. But the most intelligent dog needs training to bring out the full measure of his intelligence, and this is just what does not happen with the majority of gun-dogs. The question of the natural intelligence of the various breeds is a difficult one, and one that cannot be settled satisfactorily. Presumably the shooting dog has developed into certain breeds because those breeds are the best adapted for the purpose both physically and mentally. Presumably the best type of dog for retrieving is one of the recognised types of retriever, just as the best dog for tracking is the bloodhound. Yet the best retriever I have ever seen was a poodle. (By the way, was St. John's " poodle " really a poodle? One always sees the breed mentioned in quotation marks, signifying doubt on the part of the quoter. But having seen a poodle in action, I am not at all sure that St. John's dog was not a real poodle.) This dog, a black one, was certainly the equal of any field-trial winner I have seen, and personally I think he was superior to any died-in-the-wool retriever of my experience. And he did not belong to me! Alsatians also make excellent retrievers. And I have seen Dalmatians put up a very good show and hold their own with the recognised gun-dogs in the field. A friend of mine uses an Airedale with satisfactory results, and is experimenting with two Elkhounds, both of which will retrieve to hand as well as any true gun-dog, but both of which are as yet a little unsteady.

Any dog can be taught to retrieve. That may be unpalatable to keen shooting men; but, then, the truth is often unpalatable. Nose is something that cannot be given to a dog; he must be born with it. But most breeds are born with nose, and their scenting powers can be improved with constant practice. Courage they cannot be given; and it does require courage to face thick cover or cold water. But, given courage, I am by no means sure that it is impossible to make the most unlikely-looking dog a good gun-dog, or at any rate as good a gun-dog as the average one sees about the country.

And when it comes to intelligence—impossible as it is to propound standards—I think that it must be acknowledged that the retriever and the pointer and the setter, and even the spaniel, cannot take very high rank. One meets exceptionally intelligent members of all these breeds, of course, just as one meets exceptional members of any other breed, but the average cannot rank, in my opinion, very highly. And having gone so far, I may as well take my courage in both hands and go farther; I may as well list the dogs I regard as the most intelligent, taking their breed as a whole.

First I should place the Alsatian. The dog has an unenviable reputation. It is widely regarded as untrustworthy in temper, as likely to become savage. This is due to its appearance. The wolf-like look makes people of nervous disposition regard it as a wolf. It is, in fact, no more untrustworthy in temperament than any other breed, and a great deal less so than many. Of its intelligence there can be no doubt at all. Its use as guide-dog for the blind is proof of that. In my experience an Alsatian can be taught anything—even to being a really good gun-dog.

Second I should place the poodle. Like the Alsatian, the poodle can be taught almost anything. But their tempers are, in my experience, a little less certain than the tempers of Alsatians. On the other hand, their courage is superb. They will face the thickest cover unperturbed, and they like water. The Alsatian will face any cover if you get him young enough, but he does not relish water.

Third I should place the collie—the Scotch collie. Here again the temper is uncertain, but the courage is beyond question. Collies can be taught to retrieve perfectly, and they have the softest mouths imaginable.

All these I should place before any of the recognised gun-dog breeds in the matter of intelligence, and all can be used for the purpose. I should rank them at the top of any list of dogs in order of intelligence. Of the others, and still before any of the gun-dog breeds, I would place the Yorkshire terrier, the Pekinese, the dachshund, and the corgi. Incidentally, all these breeds are good sporting breeds when they are not spoilt. The dachshund is used in Scandinavia for hunting; the corgi can be used as a spaniel for rabbit-shooting; the Pekinese is a thorough sportsman if kept out of the reach of old ladies; and to the sporting qualities of the Yorkshire there seems to be no limit.

I

But all these are recognised breeds. There is one that receives no recognition from the Kennel Club. The lurcher must take very high rank in this matter of intelligence. I do not think that it can compare with the Alsatian, but it is, in my experience, at least the equal of the poodle, and it is, I think, the superior of the collie. All Gypsy dogs are called lurchers. The word has come to mean any long dog of doubtful appearance and savage temperament and obviously doubtful pedigree. But the true lurcher is a cross between the greyhound and the collie, and nothing else. This is a cross you can breed true, and I know several Gypsy families that do breed true lurchers from lurcher parents. It is a true breed, no matter what the Kennel Club may say. And it is a breed of truly remarkable intelligence.

The Poacher's Dog! What tales have been woven around it and its superhuman intelligence! So many tales, of such startling nature, that the true merit of the breed has become cloaked in a shroud of mythology, and all tales of its intelligence are now disbelieved. Let me quote again the writer upon the subject of poachers and poachers' dogs: "We read so much about him and his dog, that marvellous animal capable of scenting a keeper half a mile away, who will meet his master at any given point, getting there by a different route to avoid raising suspicion. The dog is said, on seeing any one approaching, to slip through the roadside fence and obliterate itself till that person has passed out of sight. According to report, no hare can escape the poacher's dog. . . ." And that is just about the usual attitude to the poacher's dog. But few poachers, I have found, use dogs much. And I have not yet found one that used a lurcher. The lurcher is not the poacher's dog. It is the Gypsy's dog.

I have seen some wonderful lurchers, all owned and trained by Gypsies. Most of these dogs have come from one of two Gypsy families that make a practice of breeding lurchers. The one family travels the Welsh border country and the other the South country (I will not be more definite than that), and their dogs have a great and deserved reputation among Gypsies the country over. But quite beyond the breeding—though that is, of course, most important—there is the question of training. The Gypsy with a hankering for good dogs takes enormous trouble over the training of his animals, and a good Romani dog-trainer has forgotten more about the training of dogs for the purpose for which he wishes to

"All Gypsies own lurchers."

use them, and more about the training of dogs generally, than any gorgio (that is, non-Gypsy) trainer has ever known. And this training is kind for the most part. By that I mean that beating is reduced to a minimum. Some beating of a dog is necessary, as every trainer will agree, and the Gypsy dog gets some beating as correction for misdemeanour. But the best Gypsy trainer of lurchers that I have ever known, and the next best, *never under any circumstances* used a stick to a dog. Both maintained that it did much more harm than good. Indeed, they went farther than that : both told me that a trainer who used a stick to a dog was no trainer at all. And certainly their dogs were better than any others I have seen, even among good Gypsy dogs.

The Gypsy who does go in for dogs—all Gypsies own lurchers, of course, and all use them, but that is rather different from going in for them thoroughly—usually breeds them himself, using the blood of one of the two strains that I have referred to, or buys them as very young puppies from one or other of the two families owning the strains. And he will never sell his dogs—not under any circumstances. Which, when one remembers the great use they are to him in so many ways, is not surprising.

I have written in two previous books about the dogs owned by James Arigho, a Romani-Tinker friend of mine. These dogs—and I have seen them at work on several occasions—seem to know exactly what their master means by every word and every gesture. And they know exactly what to do when the night's work is over. I do not know that they can " scent a keeper half a mile away ", but they never accompany him home, and they always return home separately and by different routes, and devious routes at that. How many dog-trainers can train their charges to do that?

The writer already referred to casts doubt on the ability of the poacher's dog to meet his master at a given place and to get there by a different route to avoid raising suspicion. I have never known a poacher's dog that could do that, and should be surprised to learn that any poacher possessed such a dog, or the patience to train one to that state of perfection. But for some years I have been hearing rumours from my Gypsy friends about a man in Dorset who had dogs he had trained to do so. I mentioned this man—not by name—in a previous book, describing him as a farm labourer, and being careful to stress that I had only heard rumours of his existence. For then I did not know if what I had heard was true. Since then I have met the man and his dogs. He is not a farm labourer: he is a Gypsy. And I have met his dogs and seen them work. He has four lurchers of his own breeding of the Welsh border blood. Actually he has more than this—his total kennel is eight—but the four are the ones he is using at the moment. They are, as is the case with all good poaching lurchers used by Gypsies, bitches. Dogs are used for work, of course, for they must know at least a little of the work their breed must do, but bitches are used in the main, and always for important work. Much greater store is set on the bitches than on the dogs, not only for work, but also for breeding. A Gypsy dog-fancier is not concerned, when buying a puppy, about the father so much as about the mother (which is in direct contrast to our own practice), and bitches fetch much higher prices.

But to return to this Dorset Gypsy and his four bitches. I have never seen animals trained to such a state of perfection. Arigho's dogs are good, but they are almost non-starters in comparison. It may sound unbelievable, but it is true. His dogs do meet him at given places on the road. I have seen it done, not once, not twice, but several times. I was, I admit, a bit sceptical about it before I had seen it. I was even a bit sceptical about it when I had seen it with my own eyes the first time, for I was not certain that the meeting-place was not a usual one. But half a dozen times, and each time at a different place, was convincing. As I have said, I have seen it done. But I do not know how it is done. It seemed to be done simply by a wave of the arm; but there must be more to it than that. Be that as it may, on the first occasion we were going to some woods about three miles away from the encampment. We were to meet some other Gypsy friends there at about seven o'clock in the evening. This was not a poaching expedition, but merely an expedition to show me how the dogs worked this meeting business. We left about six. The dogs were sent on about half an hour earlier. There seemed to be no more than a wave of the arm, and they were gone. We walked up a lane between high banks. There was a bend in this lane, and as we came to it, Harry said, " There is a stile about a hundred yards up. They'll be there." Just before we came to the stile one of the dogs fell in behind us. A few yards farther on and the second came down the bank just ahead of us. The third came through the stile, and the fourth joined us just after the stile had been passed. All fell in behind.

Half a mile farther on a man appeared walking towards us. Said Harry, " Have a look at the dogs." I turned round, and the dogs had vanished. " They'll always do that when they see someone they do not know," said Harry, " but if they know you are all right they won't take no notice." This rather astonishing statement I later put to the test of myself, and found to be true.

Not wholly convinced by this first expedition, I was treated to others, some of them actual poaching expeditions. On each occasion the dogs met us on the road at just the spot their master said they would, and on each occasion they left for the rendezvous some little time before us. Like Arigho's dogs, they found their own way home. Arigho's dogs will also leave should a stranger appear on the road when they are out with their master, but he has not got them to the advanced stage of being able to recognise friend from possible foe, as has Harry.

Neither man ever talks to his dogs when they are at work. All instructions are given by signs, and occasionally by low whistles, but as often as not the dogs seem to know what is required of them without any instruction being necessary. These dogs are much, much more intelligent and much better and steadier than the best of the Field Trial champions I have watched, and I have watched most of the best Field Trial champions of the last ten years or so.

Not all the abilities of the Gypsy's lurcher would be acceptable to the shooting man. But there can be no doubt that the trainer of gun-dogs—for that matter the trainer of any breed of dog—could learn a thing or two from the Gypsy dog-trainer.

Chapter XI

PARTRIDGES AND PHEASANTS

And doesn't he look dapper
　　When March is burning bright—
A perfect little scrapper,
　　A perfect little knight?
When all the world is living
　　To love and fight once more
I like to see him giving
　　The other chap " what for ".

Patrick Chalmers.

ALL true countrymen love the partridge. The little brown bird holds a position in the countryside and in the hearts of rural Englishmen that can never be usurped by the gorgeous pheasant. The partridge living has all the virtues. The partridge dead has the supreme virtue of being very good to eat. And since the taste for game is not confined to one class, it is not surprising to find that the partridge is much sought after by those who cannot afford to shoot it or buy it from the game-dealers.

The usual methods of taking the partridge are by net and by snare. A partridge-net is made of fine, strong hemp, for this is both soft and durable, and is not likely to shrink or to get tangled up when wet. It is made in a single sheet, and is generally from 20 to 30 yards long and from 12 to 14 feet deep. It is netted in a square mesh, and the meshes are 2 inches square. The top of the net is threaded on to a rope. And the use of the net is simple: it is simply trailed over the birds.

But perhaps it is not quite so simple as that, for you must first find the birds. This is done by watching them in the late evening, and by knowing something of the habits of partridges. The partridge, like the Englishman, is a creature of conservative habit. But its habits, though always conservative, change a little with the season of the year.

Before the shooting season begins they are birds of little caution. Watch them after the harvest is gathered, and you may see them in the stubble-fields playing about without a care in the world—" playing " is a word that may offend the scientific naturalist, but I know no better word to describe the manner in which they chase each other, chattering away in the happiest way the while. But once they have been shot at they develop caution. And as the season advances they become more and more cautious in their habits, and apparently, though this is not actually the case, more erratic in their movements. Early in the season they fly to their roosting-places long before dusk. But as the season ages, and they are disturbed more and more by day and by night, they very rarely leave their feeding-grounds until it is too dark to see them on the wing, and often they will run over field after field to the roosting-place.

The fact that it is essential for the poacher to know is the roosting-place. This is not so difficult to discover as might be thought. For one thing, partridges very rarely roost on a stubble-field, which is all to the good so far as the poacher is concerned, as a net drawn over stubble makes a whistling sound which will put every bird in that field and the next on the alert and give the poacher's presence away to other people if they be about as well. Stubble-fields may, therefore, be ignored. It is the other sorts of fields that matter. And here the conservative habits of the partridge save the poacher a lot of trouble. Partridges are not only very fond of certain fields to roost in, but they show a marked preference for certain parts of those fields. They stick to these fields and to the particular parts of these fields year after year. A covey may have two, or perhaps three, favourite roosting-places, using them according to the weather. But you soon get to know what sort of weather means which roosting-place. And as a matter of fact, a covey will probably not change its roosting-place more than one night in four. You can be quite definite about this. Rash as it may seem to those not conversant with the ways of partridges, I would be prepared to bet that I could find a covey in my neighbour-hood two nights out of four merely by walking to certain parts of certain fields.

"All true countrymen love the partridge."

It may be thought that this excessive conservatism on the part of the partridge is a great help to the gamekeeper in his battle with the poacher.   If partridges are scarce it is a help, of course, though not as much as one might think.   But in a partridge country it is a hindrance rather than a help.   The good keeper will know just as well as the good poacher the roosting-places of the birds, but in a well-stocked country there will be many of these roosting-places, and they cannot all be watched all night.   As always in this battle, the poacher knows where he is going, the keeper has a large tract of country to cover.   No, the conservatism of the partridge is all on the side of the poacher.

But knowing in which field and in which part of that field the covey will roost for the night is not enough.   Things look very different at night.   And though it is easy enough to flush a covey (that is, to find one and put it up—as I say, I believe that I could do that in my neighbourhood two nights out of four), what the poacher has to do is to find the covey and flush it into his net.   This means that he must mark down the covey accurately—mark it down to within a few yards.   So he watches the birds as dusk falls, and " sets " the covey.   He can, in fact, if he climbs a tree or uses some other high vantage point, " set " several coveys at once in a good partridge district.   To " set " a covey is to mark its position between two landmarks in a field.   The net is then trailed from the one mark to the other so that it covers the birds.

A moonlight night is all against the partridge poacher.   The darker the night the better, and the best night of all is when there is a slight rain falling and a steady, but not strong, wind blowing.   Moonlight nights are not beloved by poachers generally. With one exception—roosting pheasants, for which moonlight is essential—everything can be done better and safer on a moonless night.   There is one other thing that is not beloved by the poacher, and that is frosty weather.   Frost handicaps him greatly, and helps him little, if at all.   For one thing, silence is essential to success in poaching; the poacher must be as noiseless as possible.   It is by no means easy to walk silently on frozen ground.   Quite apart from this, it is not easy to work when one is cold.   And it is not easy to work quickly and quietly if one is cluttered up with thick clothing.   And should one have to run for it, much and heavy clothing is a severe handicap indeed.   There are other drawbacks, too.   If you walk over frozen ground you leave a track—a black track easily recognisable and easily followed when the sun gets up. And it is not easy to set snares in frozen ground—you can get over this by hanging your snares from fences by the string, instead of propping them up in the ground, but it is not a very satisfactory method—and netting over frozen ground is just foolish waste of time.

But to return to partridges: a night with slight rain and a steady wind is the best sort of weather for netting. The net is trailed against the wind towards the birds. By so doing the scent of the drawer is blown away from the birds as he approaches them, and any noise he may make is also carried away. Moreover, a net drawn against the wind keeps straight, and so is more easily worked. As soon as the net touches the birds, they flush. There is a sudden whirr of wings in the dark—one's heart leaps into one's mouth the first time or two—and the net is dropped. If it has been done properly, the birds will be underneath it, and all is well. Partridges in a net stay silent. Not so with other creatures. And it is sometimes extraordinary what will be taken in a partridge net of a night. An occasional pheasant—horribly noisy bird; lapwings—they are noisy, too; the odd woodcock—as silent as the partridge; but the most frequent captures, other than partridges, are larks. It is always amazing to me the number of larks that are caught in this way, and why they do not get through the meshes of the net. It is also amazing that they do not flutter about much, but seem to be content to await release without making any noise. Generally they are released. They are too small to bother about. Get the partridges and get away, is the feeling of the average poacher. But if the net is worked by Gypsies, then the larks caught are usually killed, for they are regarded as a great luxury by Gypsies as well as by those who patronise the fashionable London restaurants. Sometimes, especially in late October, rabbits are taken in the partridge nets. Then there is an awful row. The rabbit is a noisy little beast, and does his best to let the whole world know what has happened to him. A rabbit or two in the net means that the poacher must move quickly to deal with the noise. Sometimes, too, a hare is taken—but by no means as frequently as one might imagine—and the hare is also a noisy creature in a net. Moreover, a hare in a partridge net can wreak havoc. It is a powerful animal, and it does not take kindly to nets.

On a very dark night, partridges, when flushed by the net and the covey broken, will seldom leave the field in which they have roosted. They will merely leave the roosting-ground for another part of the same field. On such a night, if the poacher misses some birds with his first draw—or, as sometimes happens, misses the whole covey—he just trails his net round and round the field, and by so doing catches the lot one by one. But it must be a very dark night. On nights of average blackness the birds, if missed by the first haul, will leave for another field.

The usual method adopted by gamekeepers to prevent partridge netting is to strew some bushes, preferably thorn-bushes, here and there all over the field or fields. Some gamekeepers set great store by this method, and it is always recommended by the text-books and the gamekeeping papers. But to the experienced poacher it is only a slight, indeed only a very slight, annoyance. It certainly does not prevent an experienced man from working. It does not even hinder a really experienced man, who has got his covey properly set and has estimated the distance to be covered from his starting-point to the birds. Such a man has only to count his steps to be pretty sure of his birds. But the bushing of fields is undoubtedly a deterrent to the non-expert and the tyro, and is for that reason worth doing.

French partridges may be netted in just the same way, and with equal success. But the Frenchman is often taken by Gypsies in another and simpler way. The French partridge, as every shooting man knows, is a lazy bird, and is most averse to taking wing if it can possibly avoid doing so. There is, therefore, no need to go to the trouble of walking with a net. It is much easier, and every bit as certain, to get the birds to walk into the net. This can be done with the aid of two or three well-trained dogs. The birds must be watched into their roosting-place, and the lie of the land from that place must be carefully noted. The net must be set down-wind from the birds, and the dogs must be put in up-wind from the birds. The process is, in fact, exactly the reverse from that of walking with the net. The reasons are twofold. Firstly, the birds must scent the dogs; and secondly, they must not find anything to encourage them to take wing. Birds, like aeroplanes, prefer to take off into the wind. But into the wind in this case means into the dogs, and the French partridge would always prefer to run if that is the case. Furthermore, they are not sure that there is really any danger. They will not move until the dogs are almost on top of them, and then they start to run away from the dogs, but not too fast, for they are not sure that the dogs are really after them, and they do not want to go too far from the roost if there is not really any need to do so. Two well-trained lurchers are sufficient to do the job thoroughly, but three are better, for then there is less chance of any of the birds running out. I have seen some remarkable work done by a team of lurchers. I have seen some remarkable work done by a single lurcher, for that matter. And not the least remarkable feature has been the way in which the dogs have refused to be distracted by hares or rabbits which they may have put up on the way to the net. Yet the same dogs may be used the next night for hares. How they are trained in this manner and to this state of perfection I do not yet know, but I hope to find out some day. At any rate, the Gypsy's lurcher seems to understand exactly what it is he is required to do on a partridge night, just as he understands what is required on a hare night.

The partridge is also very easy to snare. The snares used for this purpose are made of the finest catgut. Here again the conservative habits of the bird are put to good use by the poacher. Partridges are very fond of dust-baths on a fine morning. And they have a habit of going regularly to the same place for their bath. The places they like best are hedge-slips where the soil is fine and dry. The nooses are laid in the loose mould, and when the birds begin to scratch in the soil they are soon caught by the feet. Quite a number are also caught by the head, presumably as they put their heads down to the soil at the end of the bath. A great many birds are taken in this way. But it was the Italian prisoners working on our farms that really reduced the business of partridge snaring to a fine art. Their snares were beautifully made, though they must have found it hard to get decent material, and the men were expert at setting the snares in the right places. They also placed them in the soil, as our English poachers do, but they went further than that, and used to get the birds as they ran through the hedges to the slips, snaring them by the neck and strangling them instantaneously. To set a snare so is truly an expert's work. Many of our Italian prisoners were experts.

Pheasants are not netted. Occasionally one appears in a partridge net, but no practice is made of netting them. Most pheasants are taken by stoving, and some very large hauls are made in this way. A stove is canister-shaped with a perforated top. At the bottom there is a sliding drawer, and immediately above this there is a false bottom, and this is also perforated. The stove is filled with sulphur, and in the drawer there is placed an oiled rag or anything that will burn slowly. The poacher fixes the stove to a long pole, lights the rag or whatever it may be in the drawer, and then holds the stove up right under the bird on its roosting-perch. The bird is in a few moments stupefied by the sulphur fumes and topples from its perch, to be instantly pounced upon and despatched. It must be taken at once, for the effect of the sulphur does not last for more than a few seconds. The best sort of night for this kind of job is one on which the moon is bright in a cloudless sky. The birds can then easily be seen as they roost. Frosty nights are no good, for too much noise is made in approaching the birds, and a night with any wind is also no good, for the wind will blow the smoke from under the birds. For the job to be done properly the smoke must get all around the birds.

Of course, there are men who use a gun on roosting pheasants. Even men who in the normal course of events would never dream of using a gun give way to temptation where pheasants are concerned. But it is a risky business, and a good poacher—by that I mean a man who is not a member of a gang, but a man who poaches for his food and for sport—will not take the risk. If you are prepared to take the risk of being found with a gun, and perhaps put to the evil temptation of using it to avoid capture, then there is nothing easier, I should think, than to brown pheasants at roost. But that is a form of procedure for which I have no room at all.

There are other and better ways of dealing with pheasants at roost. A catapult, for instance, is a deadly weapon in the hands of an expert. I have seen some experts with a catapult—in my youth I was no mean hand at the job myself—but the catapult has this disadvantage, that you can only take one bird at a time. True, if you are really good you will be able to get two or even three birds from one perch before the others have woken up to what is going on, but there are not many men as expert as that.

And then there is the whip. The best poacher I have ever known, a Gypsy, always used a whip, when the night was really bright with the moon and the ground was not frostbound. He could use a catapult as well as any man I have known, and he knew most sorts of ways of getting game out of the night. But the whip was his favourite method: not because he got bigger bags that way, for he did not, but because it needed real skill, and so provided real sport. The whip has a very short handle and a very long thong. Arigho, a deadly shot with a gun or a catapult, was as deadly with this whip. I have seen him bring down a roosting pheasant from its perch, and so silently that he had the next off the perch before it was aware that its neighbour had disappeared. That does require skill. If you do not believe it, go out and try on your own pheasants. You may be pleased if you can get under them without disturbing them. Indeed, you may well be pleased with yourself if you can get within ten yards of them without sending the whole lot crashing the wood.

Chapter XII

RABBITS

Perhaps my cave-man blood's to blame
For—atavistic taint—I too
Have dropped a more exacting game,
Bunny, to have a bang at you;
The driven partridge missed in front,
And eke behind, lacks serious merit,
Beside a sunny hedgerow hunt,
A terrier and an active ferret!

Patrick Chalmers.

THE rabbit is, so to speak, the bread-and-butter of the poacher. The ways of getting the rabbit are legion, and range from the shot-gun through the trap and the snare (and simply knocking it over with a stick in a hedgerow) to the use of nets. But of all the hundred and one ways of getting the rabbit, only those involving the use of nets are, I think, of real interest.

Nets are of two kinds: the long net and the purse net. A long net is usually made 50 yards long. It is netted in just the same way as the purse net—that is, the ordinary net used for ferreting—and it is strung in just the same manner. The meshes of a long net are 2 inches square, and it is always made 14 meshes wide. Indeed, except for size, the only difference between the long net and the purse net is that the former requires about 80 yards of sarking to be strung on two strings of about 50 yards each. It is, by the way, much better to have too much sarking in a net than too little.

The method of working the net is also simple. To the ends of the strings at each end of the net there is attached an iron pin about a foot long, and the net is gathered up on to one of these pins. But these pins are not enough by themselves to keep upright a net 50 yards long when it is stretched out, so when a net is run out along a woodside or along a hedgerow it is kept upright by means of sticks. Each stick is about 18 inches in height, and they are stuck into the ground about ten paces apart. The string that runs through the top of the net is wound round the tops of the sticks, and the string that runs through the bottom of the net is wound round the bottom of each stick—two or three times round each stick—and a net so set should stand firmly and quite upright. When a rabbit runs into such a net it immediately gets entangled in the midst of the quantity of loose sarking in the spaces between the sticks, and the more it struggles the more it becomes entangled. In a well-constructed net it will soon be so entangled that it cannot move at all.

But, though the use of the long net is so simple, one has got to know a good deal about the rabbit and its habits to use it successfully. The rabbit is a nervous creature and, though one does hear occasionally of a rabbit attacking a stoat or a weasel and bowling it over, such occurrences are very rare and are given a prominence that they do not deserve. The rabbit is, in fact, an animal that will not fight any but its own kind, and then only under pronounced sexual stimulus, an animal that will not fight even in defence of its own life. It is gifted with a very keen sense of smell, and a very considerable turn of speed over a short distance, and it relies on these two qualities to save it from danger. Especially at night does it rely on its sense of smell, and a moderately acute sense of hearing.

The man who would work a long net successfully at night must make full allowance for these two qualities of the rabbit. He must make sure that the wind is in his favour. If it blows from him over the rabbits before he has his nets set, his chances of catching any are poor indeed. If it blows from him over the rabbits and to the net after he has the net set, then so much the better. But he must be very careful to see that his quarry does not get a scent of him until the nets are set, and this is not by any means as easy as it may sound, for one outlier can spoil a whole night's work. Rabbits are gregarious animals. All gregarious animals are easily startled; when one is startled and begins to run, the infection spreads as rapidly as the plague, and all will take it that the frightened animal is in imminent danger, and will begin to run also. The least alarm is enough to set every rabbit in a large area on the move at night. And this applies equally to noise. The least noise is

K

sufficient to alarm the lot. So the man who would enjoy a successful night with the long net must tread carefully. A step on a dry
and rotten stick, the kicking of a loose stone, and a night's work
may well be ruined. The quietest way to walk is not on tip-toe,
but on the heel of the foot first.

And then the weather must be studied. It is no good trying
the long net during frosty weather. For one thing, it is not easy
to drive the sticks into the ground during a frost, and if the sticks
are not set up, the long net is not much use. And for another,
rabbits rarely feed by night during a frost. A very dark night is
not much good either. On very dark nights rabbits do not move
far from their home. And a bright moonlight night is also not
much good, except, perhaps, on the very tops of the downs. On a
bright moonlight night a man is easily seen, and an outlier is almost
certain to give the alarm before he has had a chance to set his nets.
A wet night is also useless. Rabbits have an aversion to getting
wet, and do not come out on a wet night. Again, I have found
that a night of east wind is unfavourable. Rabbits seem to have
as great a dislike for the east wind as the average human. A north
wind is not so bad, but it is unlikely, in my experience, that a really
good bag will be made on a night of north wind. The best winds
are those from the south or west. And the best of all is a steady
wind from the south, for this dries the dew, and makes the working
of the nets easier. Also, for some reason, rabbits seem to be less
on the alert when the south wind is blowing. I do not know if
there is any scientific reason for this. I suspect that the scientists
would laugh at the idea. But that it is so I am quite convinced
from personal experience, and I know that it has been the experience of others also. Incidentally, it also applies to sheep.

There is an idea that it is necessary to have a dog to drive rabbits
into the long net. This is not so. A dog is an advantage where
hares are concerned, but where rabbits are the quarry a dog is, if
anything, a handicap. It is very much harder to train a dog to
keep quiet about a rabbit, and when, as is usually the case, there are
several rabbits all at once even the best of dogs becomes a little
excited and starts to yelp. The expert with the long net never uses
a dog. Rabbits can be driven better, and in silence, with the aid
of a rope. A rope about 150 yards in length is used, and it is trailed
across the field by two men, one on each side of the field. The men
do not walk, they run as briskly as they can in the dark. The rope,

as it passes over the ground, makes a continual *swish, swish, swish,* and this sets every living thing in the field on the move.

The reactions of the various creatures disturbed by the rope are interesting. The rabbits, of course, make for their burrows, and are intercepted by the net. Hares will be taken by the net, too, on occasion. It is the reactions of other animals and birds that are interesting, and these reactions should be noticed by any one who wishes to become expert in the use of the long net.

Lapwings usually rise long before the rope has reached them and fly away with a scream. Partridges rise with a sudden whirr of wings, but usually circle immediately and settle in the same field. Skylarks twitter, and from the hedgerows, if the men be near enough to them, hundreds of finches and yellow-hammers and buntings burst out and circle and return to the same hedge behind the rope.

There remain the domestic animals. Horses are the worst. No man in his senses will try to work a field in which there are horses. As soon as they find a man in their field they start to gallop about, and they neigh and generally make a dreadful noise, and of course they startle every rabbit in the neighbourhood, and they startle other creatures as well—gamekeepers, for instance. Horses are easily frightened. Cows, on the other hand, are not easily frightened. But they are incurably curious. If they find a man in their field, they will follow him all over the place. If they see a net set, they will walk up and sniff at it in the most inquisitive manner. This does not matter so long as they do not get entangled in it, and this, fortunately, they rarely do. Nor are they frightened by the swish of the rope across the ground, as horses are. They are startled when first they hear it. They stare at the ground and twitch their tails about, but they do not move. When the rope touches them, they jump sideways, and then run a few paces backwards. Then the rope touches them again, and they usually jump into the air, the rope passes under them, and immediately they will forget about it, or in some cases will turn round and follow it. I do not know if it is a recognised fact that some breeds of cattle are more curious than others. Farmers I have talked to about this do not appear to have noticed any difference in the degree of curiosity displayed by their cattle generally, though they were inclined to think that if such a difference existed, it would be the Guernsey that was the most curious. But any one who has worked a long net at night and taken any interest in the reactions of the domestic animals he has disturbed will know that there is a remarkable difference in the degree of inquisitiveness shown by the various breeds of cattle. By far the most curious is the Guernsey. Almost all Guernseys will turn and follow the rope after it has passed under them. Next, in my experience, comes the redpoll; most redpolls will turn and follow the rope, at any rate for a few paces. The most incurious is the shorthorn. Once the net has been inspected they lose interest, and once the rope has passed them they forget it. Once an Aberdeen Angus was so interested in the behaviour of a friend of mine that it was not content with following the rope to see what happened, but it stayed around and watched the haul being stowed away, and then insisted on following the men out of the field. This became embarrassing, and finally the animal had to be beaten off.

Sheep, strangely enough, are no trouble to the poacher at night. They are frightened, of course. They are gregarious, and one startled means the flock startled. But when disturbed at night sheep scarcely ever bleat. They gallop about to avoid the rope, but they usually do so in a circle, and so rarely come into contact with the net, and once the rope is past them they gallop off to the other end of the field and stand huddled together. Sheep can see pretty well in the dark, for they always seem to be able to jump the rope at the right moment, while cows have to wait until it has touched them, and then leap straight upwards like acrobats.

Hares are seldom caught in the long nets. This is because the long net is usually set along the side of a wood or a hedgerow. A rabbit disturbed at night will take to the shelter of a wood, but a hare will never do so. And if the net is set along a hedgerow, and the hare is pressed by dogs, it will invariably jump over the net, and not infrequently over the hedge also. If you want to get hares by the long net you will never set the net in the field where the hares are feeding, but always outside it—behind the hedge or behind a gate. And if you do this you will not get any rabbits. So hares taken in the long net—and they are so taken occasionally— are taken by accident, and not by skill.

Long netting should never be done before midnight. The best catches are always made just before dawn. Rabbits stray a good distance during a night, but they always come back to the fields near their burrows and to fields near woods before the dawn, and it is then that they may be best encouraged into the nets.

Purse-netting is, of course, quite a different technique. For one thing, you must have ferrets. You can do without everything else—except the nets—but you cannot do without ferrets.

Ferreting, curiously enough, does not come under the heading of "sport". Heaven knows why; but it is so. Your true sportsman looks down upon ferreting, and so, of course, also looks down upon the man who ferrets. I found that out long ago. The true sportsman does not frown upon ferrets—very far from that—and he certainly does not disdain their use. A number of ferrets, six guns or so, and a good lunch: I do not know the sportsman who would say "no" to such a day. But that is not ferreting. Nor is it sport. It is pleasure. And ferreting should properly be regarded as a job of work. It is a means by which rabbits may be kept down, it is a means of killing rabbits, and if it needs six guns and a good lunch, it is a ridiculously expensive means. Ferreting should always be good fun, but it should never be expensive. And there is not the slightest reason why it should ever be expensive. The number of burrows where even two guns are necessary are very few, and personally I consider that one gun is quite enough, and I am certain that it is the best number. One gun means no talking—and talking is a waste of time—means that there is no need for politeness (which means better shooting and a better chance of shooting), and also means less digging, for with one gun far fewer rabbits are hit behind. It is astonishing how many rabbits are hit behind in a six-gun party. For ferreting with a gun, I think that, besides the man with the gun, all that is necessary is a man with a spade, half a dozen purse-nets, three loose ferrets and a good line ferret. That is not an expensive team, but it can be a very efficient one. If you think that it is an expensive one, then you can dispense with the man with the spade and do your own digging. You will get plenty of exercise that way, and if you know the job you will get quite a few rabbits also.

But the best of all methods of ferreting is with the nets alone and without a gun. This is called "poachers' business" by some people (who know nothing about poaching), and it is called by all sportsmen sheer murder, and no sport at all. Strangely enough, the people who know nothing about poaching are right; it is poachers' business, it is the way good poachers work the purse-nets. As to its being murder and not sport, that does not matter at all. I do not mind how many rabbits are murdered. They deserve no better end. And it is sport. I know no better sport than the skilful use of the purse-net without the aid of a gun.

Successful ferreting of this sort requires more than a fair knowledge of woodcraft and an inexhaustible store of patience. Without these two essentials, the day or the night will almost certainly degenerate into a day or a night of digging. It also needs the right sort of ferret, the right sort of dog, and the right sort of companion, for a companion is absolutely necessary for this type of ferreting.

On the right sort of ferret there is endless argument. Personally, I prefer small white ferrets. I do not like polecat ferrets for rabbiting—though for ratting there is nothing to beat them—because they are hard enough to see in daylight, and quite impossible to see at night, and because I think that they are too fast and savage. A polecat becomes a killer on the slightest provocation, and has a great tendency to lie up with his rabbit, and that means a lot of digging—an amusement I very soon get tired of. I like small white ferrets for a number of reasons. Because they have not, as a rule, the strength to pin down and hold a rabbit, because they can, owing to their small size, get past a rabbit at the end of a passage and drive it out, when a big ferret would be tempted to kill or to lie up; and because they are easily handled and quite tame. I never mind putting my hand down a hole to drag out a rabbit held by a small white ferret. I have been bitten, of course, but it has been my own fault for making a sudden movement, and the bite has never been serious. The bite of a big polecat, on the other hand, is not a pleasant experience.

There is also endless argument about the best methods of working ferrets. Personally I do not believe in starving a ferret for twenty-four hours before working. This is the common practice, but I do not think that a hungry ferret really works any faster than a fed ferret. On the other hand, I do believe that a hungry ferret unmuzzled will try to kill, and if it does kill it will certainly lie up and feed. I am a great believer in working ferrets unmuzzled, and I have found that a fed ferret very rarely kills, and if it does kill it still more rarely lies up. There is another point, too. A fed ferret, if it should not come to the surface within a reasonable space of time, can generally be cajoled into doing so. There are a number of ways of doing this. I find a soft whistle most efficacious myself:

but, then, I always give a soft whistle before feeding my ferrets, and they know what it means. If it fails—and it rarely does so—I have never known the smoke of dead bracken wafted down the hole to fail. And lastly, a muzzled ferret loses half the power of bolting.

Personally I like to use small jills, and I like to use them without lines. I am not keen on lines. A line, besides having a tendency to get hung up, very easily tires a small ferret, and I do not think that a line is necessary if the ferret is at all easy to handle. But I always have a big buck to use as a line ferret if necessary.

There is also some argument as to the best way to carry your ferrets. Some men prefer boxes, and some prefer sacks. Myself, I prefer a sack. And if you are going to work at night, a sack is essential, for a box is an awkward thing to carry if you are in a hurry. But there is little purse-netting done at night, though it can be quite effective if done before midnight. Those who object to sacks say that a sack becomes damp when laid on the ground, and is draughty if hung up in a tree, and that both damp and draughts are bad for the health of ferrets. I cannot say that I have ever found that the health of my ferrets has suffered. Ferrets are really extremely hardy, and their health suffers only if they are pampered, and that, I find, is the general tendency of ferret-owners. My ferrets are treated pretty roughly so far as comforts are concerned, and they thrive. I cannot pronounce upon the merits of a box, as I have never used one. But I should expect ferrets in a box to be pretty noisy. And silence is absolutely essential to successful purse-netting.

Then there is the dog. Most people favour terriers for this sort of work. I have never yet found a terrier that I consider a good dog for purse-netting rabbits. The dog should have a very good nose, and he should be able to mark rabbits underground reliably. He must have no tendency to bark or snort down holes, and he must not wish to dig or scratch. He must be silent. That is the one golden rule for this sort of ferreting—utter and complete silence. If you can find those qualities in a dog—and they are not easy to find—then it does not matter in the least what breed he is or is not.

Having got your dog, and he having marked the holes for you, you place your nets in position. Each net must be carefully counted, for it is dreadfully easy to overlook a net in the darkness of a winter's evening, and a net once left is not easily found again. The nets in position, the ferret should be dropped very quietly at the entrance to the hole, and the net held firmly so that it may pass through without getting tangled up and without disturbing or dragging the net.

Netting rabbits without a gun is a really thrilling business. For one thing, you have to be so utterly silent. Rabbits have the most amazing powers of hearing, and anything but the lightest of steps will warn a whole burrow. You must be stealthy and cat-like in your approach, and that is not always easy. You must trim back the brambles and the bracken to make room for the purse-nets, and the nets must be laid accurately. And all this must be done as silently as may be, and that in itself is an exciting business, for man is a clumsy animal. And then, all the preparations having been made, you insert the ferret and sit back and wait. You must sit out of sight of the hole—out of sight of all the holes if you can, but that is the counsel of perfection—and to leeward, and you wait. Usually you do not have to wait long. But it always seems a very long time indeed, and the suspense adds to the excitement. Then suddenly—and really it will be only a matter of a moment or two since the ferret was inserted—there will be the faint thud of the warning stamp deep down in the burrow. Then comes a rumble, muffled but growing louder and clearer as it approaches the entrance to the hole, a last swift rush . . . and there is a rabbit in the net, and the net is rolled up, and everything is fur and flurry. No suspense now: everything is happening at once. You have to act very quickly and very quietly. You must jump to the hole and seize the netted rabbit, and shove one foot into the entrance to prevent another rabbit bolting from the same hole—I have never yet seen two rabbits caught in one purse-net; but I have known more than one to follow another from the hole too quickly for the man outside—and you must kill the rabbit (that is easily done), and you must put another purse-net into the place. And pretty well you have got to do that, all of it, in two movements, and silently. If you stamp or stumble or fumble your kill you will probably spoil a good burrow's catch. Having done it all, you retire to your sitting place, and while you wait for another rabbit to bolt, you unravel the net from the first, so that you may have it ready to use again.

But rabbits do not come to the surface singly as often as one could wish. Very often they come so quickly that several nets are filled at once, and then the follow-ons are lost. And, of course, one usually overlooks a hole, or even two or three. It is not at all easy to find every exit to a burrow; indeed, I should be inclined to doubt whether one ever succeeds in doing so. And an overlooked hole means that several rabbits will escape before one can block it or net it. And then there are the occasions when a rabbit will refuse to bolt and one of the ferrets lies up with it. Always give your ferret half an hour before you commence to dig. If you can, give him an hour. Risky, of course, if you are on someone else's ground, but the good poacher will take a lot of risk to avoid losing a good ferret, and perhaps the risk is not so great, for he would not be purse-netting at all if he had not a good idea of the whereabouts of the keeper. A good line ferret should give you the right position to dig, and a good dog will tell you the shortest line of approach. But if digging is going to be attended with too much risk, then come back to the spot about six hours later, and you will probably find your ferret outside the hole down which he went originally. That advice was given me by a poacher of great experience, and I have found it to be true.

And the best time for purse-netting? There is an old saying in my part of the world to the effect that when the nuts can be shaken from the trees, the rabbits bolt best. I have no doubt that it is true—old country sayings of that kind invariably are—but it is somewhat too comprehensive for my liking. I believe that the best time for ferreting is the latter half of December and the whole of January. Before December there are too many small rabbits, and after January they are too wild. And the best time of the day is the evening—say, from half-past three of a December afternoon, taking Greenwich time, of course. Night netting of rabbits with purse-nets must be done before midnight, preferably not before ten o'clock, and it is not much good doing any after the first half of December. Young rabbits do not seem to go out much at night in late November and early December, but they grow up very quickly after that.

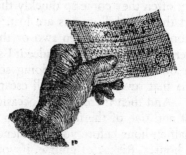

Chapter XIII

THE GAME LAWS

A Justice with grave Justices shall sit,
He praise their wisdom, they admire his wit.
No greyhound shall attend the tenant's pace,
No rusty gun the farmer's chimney grace;
Salmons shall leave their covers void of fear,
Nor dread the thievish net or triple spear;
Poachers shall tremble at his awful name,
Whom vengeance now o'ertakes for murder'd game.

John Gay.

IT is commonly said that the Game Laws take their origin from
the ancient Forest Laws, which date back at least to the days of
King Cnut. From the Norman Conquest, and for a great many
years, the right to kill game was a Royal prerogative. At first the
Crown granted the right to certain of its subjects, but gradually
the occupier of the land, by virtue of his occupancy, became
entitled to all the game killed on his soil. There were exceptions
to this, of course—the rights in a Royal Forest or Chase, for
example, and the right of Free Warren—but they are not important.
What is important is that the property in game, by custom if not
by actual grant, came to belong to the landowner. And, since the
landowner often owned land in many parts of the country, the right
to kill the game passed to the occupier. There are still plenty of
people who maintain that the occupation of land should carry with
it an unqualified right to shoot any game that may be found upon it.

That, by the way, is still legally the position in Ireland and Scotland. In England and Wales, however, the Game Act, 1831,
abolished all property qualification for entitling people to kill game,

and allowed any one to kill game provided that the requisite duty has been paid to the Inland Revenue and that permission has been obtained to go on to the land. The Game Act, 1831, is the Act in force to-day.

What is game? For the purposes of the Game Act, 1831, the following are game: hares, pheasants, partridges, grouse, heath or moor game, blackgame, and bustards. Bustards are extinct in Britain. What " heath or moor game " may be I do not know, nor, I fancy, does any one else. To shoot any of the above a game licence is necessary. This is the duty paid to the Inland Revenue.

A game licence is also necessary to shoot woodcock, snipe, quail, landrail, conies (conies are rabbits), and deer. But woodcock, snipe, quail, landrail, conies, and deer are not game. Legally you must have a game licence to shoot them. But legally they are not game.

Swans, geese, wild duck, teal, wigeon, and capercaillie are not game. And it is not necessary to have a game licence to shoot them. For protection these birds come under the provisions of the Wild Birds' Protection Acts. Woodcock and snipe, for the shooting of which it is necessary to have a game licence, also come under the Wild Birds' Protection Acts.

Deer, though they are not legally game, require a game licence before they may be taken or killed (otherwise than by hunting with hounds), except on enclosed lands, when they may be killed by the owner of the land or the occupier or his licensee. But deer are included with " game " under the Agricultural Holdings Acts in all questions of compensation for damage.

Hares are legally game. Rabbits are not. But you must have a game licence before you may shoot rabbits. Yet rabbits are not included in the enactments regarding close seasons for the killing of game. And, further, hares, which are legally game, are included with rabbits, which legally are not game, in the provisions of the Ground Game Act.

It is all very muddling. And the more you study it the more muddling does it become. It is very easy to become confused on the question of what is and what is not game. The longer you study them the more and more obvious does it become that the Game Laws are crammed full of contradictions. It is said that it takes a good lawyer to fit any given state of facts into the appropriate legal setting. It would be equally true to say that any good lawyer would have but little difficulty in circumventing the Game Laws.

The law regarding close seasons is not much better so far as clarity is concerned. Partridges may not be killed between 1st February and 1st September; pheasants between 1st February and 1st October; grouse between 10th December and 12th August; blackgame (except in Devonshire, Somerset, and in the New Forest) between 10th December and 20th August. The penalty for infringement is a fine not exceeding £1 for every head of game killed. The same penalty applies in the case of duck and geese, the close season for which is from 1st February to 11th August, though these birds are not covered by the Game Acts, but by the Wild Birds' Protection Acts, which means that the prosecution, if any, comes under a different proceeding. Furthermore, the Wild Birds' Protection Acts are subject to much variation in different districts. The penalty of a fine not exceeding £1 for every head of game killed does not apply to all the birds pursued by shooting men, but only to the birds listed above. It does not apply, for example, to the woodcock, nor to the snipe, nor to the capercaillie. There is an additional penalty of a fine not exceeding £5 for killing hares, pheasants, partridges, and grouse on a Sunday or on Christmas Day in England and Wales (this provision was withdrawn during the recent war as a temporary measure), but this does not apply to Scotland. It is also not generally realised that game are legally protected from one hour after sunset to one hour before sunrise throughout the year, so far as shooting is concerned. This applies also to ground game. It should also be remembered that the provisions of the Wild Birds' Protection Acts extend to hawks and other predatory birds, all of which receive legal protection during some portion of the year, and many of which are legally protected *throughout* the year.

Let us first consider the question of licences. The Game Act, 1831, abolished the right of the occupier to kill the wild birds and beasts he found on the land he occupied, and allowed any one who had paid a duty to the Inland Revenue (in return for which he received a game licence) to shoot game, provided that he had obtained permission to go on to the land in search of it. These licences are obtainable at almost every post office. They cost

£3 from July 31st to July 31st;
£2 from July 31st to October 31st;

£2 from October 31st to July 31st;
£1 for a fortnight.

They are not retrospective. They must therefore be obtained *before* any shooting of game is done. No one (unless he is a member of the Royal Family, or a gamekeeper appointed by the Forestry Commission—and there are one or two other, but unimportant, exceptions) may legally shoot game unless he has paid this duty and received a licence in return. The licence, by the way, does more than entitle the possessor to shoot game: it also entitles him to sell game to a licensed dealer in game.

It must not be thought that it is necessary to have a game licence to shoot. That is not the case. It is only necessary to have a game licence to shoot game, and woodcock, snipe, quail, landrail, rabbits and deer—none of which is legally game. With the exception of these creatures you only require a gun licence if you wish to shoot. The price is ten shillings for a full year (even an air-gun requires a gun licence), and for this ten shillings you can go out and shoot all sorts of things, provided you have permission to go on to the land and provided you do not infringe the close seasons or the provisions of the Wild Birds' Protection Acts. For example, ducks, geese, swans and capercaillie require only a ten-shilling licence. Finally, it is not necessary to have a licence to own a gun. It is only necessary to have a licence to *use* a gun. And there is an exception even to that. You do not have to have a licence to use a gun " in a dwelling-house or the curtilage thereof ". The curtilage does not mean the " grounds ". It is, I understand, a very restricted area, but I do not know that it has ever been defined in a court of law in a shooting case.

Now, an owner is allowed by law to shoot game on his own land. If he grants the right to shoot to somebody else but continues to occupy the land, then he has the concurrent right to shoot the ground game. If he lets the land to a tenant and does not reserve the right to the shooting, then the tenant will legally enjoy the shooting. If he does reserve the right to the shooting, he must make it very clear in the deed just what it is he is reserving, for reservations in deeds are construed strictly, and against those in whose favour they are drawn. For instance, if the owner reserves the right to shoot game, then game is all he will get, and the tenant will get the rest. Game, you will remember, consists of hares, pheasants, partridges, grouse and blackgame, and *nothing else*. A reservation to shoot game will not include woodcock, snipe, quail, rabbits or deer, for though it is necessary to have a game licence to shoot them, they are not legally game. Nor will a reservation to shoot game include wild duck or geese. It is said that the reservation of the right of " shooting and sporting " will cover everything—I do not know that that has ever been tested in the face of a good counsel—but it is obviously safer for the owner to name individually the creatures he wishes to reserve for his own shooting.

In any case, the occupier has an inalienable right to kill the ground game on the land in his occupation. If he ceases to occupy by sub-letting, then the right passes to the sub-lessee. The right can be exercised by the occupier and by those persons he has authorised in writing. These persons must be members of his household resident on the land in his occupation, or persons in his service or in regular service on the land, or any other person *bona fide* employed by him for reward in the taking of ground game. But he may authorise only one person (in addition to himself) to kill game by means of firearms. If, however, he has, apart from the provisions of the Ground Game Acts, full powers to kill rabbits —if he has not signed any agreement to the contrary—he can invite any number of people to shoot.

A shooting tenant is in rather a different position. He may acquire the right to shoot either from the owner of the land or from the tenant to whom the owner has transferred his rights either expressly or merely by failing to reserve. The right to shoot is called in law a *profit à prendre*—that is, an incorporeal hereditament of the same genus as a right of way—and it needs to be dealt with by writing under seal to make it legally effective. A right of shooting is only a right over the land as it exists at the time. It does not prevent the owner from developing the land, even should that development be to the prejudice of the shooting tenant. Furthermore, the shooting tenant must use his rights reasonably. He must not walk over standing corn, nor must he work a field of roots so frequently as to injure the crop. In a yearly tenancy of shooting rights it is only necessary to give reasonable notice. Apart from any special provisions that may be made, a six-months' notice to quit cannot be claimed.

It is common to find various clauses or provisions inserted in agreements for shooting rights. A game limit is often set (a very wise precaution), and clauses are sometimes inserted to ensure that the tenant keeps down rabbits, or maintains a stock of partridges in a certain way, or that the lessor shall reduce the amount of the rent payable should he cut timber or undergrowth in a manner prejudicial to the shooting. Other clauses sometimes inserted are to the effect that the tenant shall not kill hen pheasants after a certain date, or that he shall preserve foxes and allow hunting, or that he shall keep down vermin, or that he shall not sub-let his rights without the consent of the lessor, or that he shall indemnify the lessor against damage by game under the Agricultural Holdings Acts.

There have been a number of Agricultural Holdings Acts, the most recent having been passed in 1923. Under them an agricultural tenant is entitled to compensation for damage to his crops by game (for the purposes of this Act deer are included as game) in cases where the right to kill the game is not vested in the tenant or anybody claiming under him, other than the landlord, and he has not permission in writing to kill it. The damage must exceed one shilling an acre, and the amount, failing agreement, may be determined by arbitration, but notice in writing must be given by the tenant without delay. When the right to kill is vested in some person other than the landlord, then the landlord is entitled to be indemnified by that person against all claims for compensation. In addition to all this, there is, of course, the Ground Game Act, which gives the occupier the inalienable right to kill ground game on the land in his occupation.

While none of this is as muddled or contradictory as the Game Act itself, it is, since it is based on the Game Act, muddled and contradictory enough. Special efforts have, therefore, been made to protect shooting rights. These protective measures are two-fold, since both civil and criminal remedies are provided, though both remedies cannot be used by the same person for the same offence—at least so far as the pursuit of game by day is concerned. He must make up his mind which remedy he wishes to use.

So far as the civil remedy is concerned, the breaking of another man's close gives a right of action at Common Law in which an injunction can be sought to restrain further trespass and damages. A trespasser may be removed if he refuses to leave the land, and sufficient force may be used for that purpose. This is, however, a dangerous business—sufficient force being a matter of opinion—

and a counter-action for assault may result. In any case, the Law of Trespass is a highly technical one, especially where boundary questions are concerned. One or two examples will not be out of place in this connection. For instance, if you are shooting and you enter your neighbour's land to gather a bird which, before you shot at it, was in, or rising from, your neighbour's land, you commit a trespass. If, however, you wait a day and then go on to your neighbour's land to gather the birds or beasts killed during the shoot of the previous day, you will not be committing a trespass. Again, if a bird rises on your own land and you shoot it in the air over your neighbour's land, you can go and pick it up, and, provided it is dead, you will not be committing a trespass. But if it is not dead, but is merely wounded, then you will be committing a trespass. But if it is so severely wounded that it cannot escape, you will not be committing a trespass. How you are to tell this without going on to your neighbour's land, I do not know. And the law does not tell you.

Criminal remedies cover poaching by day and poaching by night. Poaching by day—that is, trespass by day in pursuit of game—can be proceeded against by both the actual occupier of the land and by the shooting tenant. (In the case of the civil remedy this is not so: the shooting tenant in that case would have to join the occupier in bringing the action.) Any trespasser by day in pursuit of game can be fined £2. Five or more trespassers together can be fined £5 each, merely for entering or being on the land for that purpose. If a trespasser by day in pursuit of game refuses to quit and to give his name and address, he can be arrested and conveyed before a Justice, and he may be fined up to £5 and costs. But he must be brought before the Justice within twelve hours. If he is not, he can be proceeded against by summons or warrant. If five or more trespassers by day, any of them being armed with a gun, use violence to prevent an authorised person from approaching to warn them off, they can each be fined £5 and costs.

Poaching by night is regarded more seriously. The Night Poaching Acts operate between the first hour after sunset and the last hour before sunrise. They provide that any person unlawfully taking any game or rabbits on any land, public road or footpath, or at the outlets from such land, or unlawfully entering land with a gun or other instrument to take game, is liable, upon conviction before two Justices, to three months' hard labour, and, if

he then fails to find sureties, to six months' hard labour, with
an ascending scale for subsequent offences. There are further
penalties for assault with violence, and for the case of three or more
men, any one of whom has a gun, entering by night on land.
Severe penalties they are, too.

Furthermore, the law gives power to gamekeepers—incidentally,
gamekeepers appointed by Lords of the Manor have special powers,
but these are rapidly falling into disuse—to require any one doing
any act on his employer's land for which a game licence is necessary
to produce such licence, and, on refusal, to give name and address
and place of issue of licence. A gamekeeper has power also to
require a trespasser on his employer's land in pursuit of game to
give his name and address, and on refusal to do either of these
things, to apprehend him and to take him before a Justice. A
gamekeeper has also the power to demand from any one whom
he finds on his employer's land, either by day or night, in possession
of recently killed game, the delivery up of such game and, upon
refusal, to seize it. But he must *see the game actually in the man's
possession*. A gamekeeper has *no right to search any one on suspicion*.
He has, however, power to arrest and hand over to the police any
one found on his employer's land at night for the purpose of taking
or destroying game or rabbits. This power of arrest is granted
only to the gamekeepers employed by owners or occupiers. A
gamekeeper employed by a shooting tenant has no power of
arrest.

Finally, by the Poaching Prevention Act the police are given
the power of search over persons suspected of poaching and found
by them on a highway, street, or public place. This power of
search covers also the taking of the eggs of partridges, pheasants,
grouse, and blackgame. It does not cover the eggs of swans or
ducks. But under Section 24 of the Game Act any person who
has not got the right to kill the game on the land, who takes the
eggs of any bird of game or any swan, wild duck, teal, or wigeon,
or has their eggs in his house or shop, shall upon conviction before
two Justices pay a penalty not exceeding five shillings for each
egg.

There, as briefly and as plainly as I can put it, is the law—the
law in relation to game and the laws designed to protect the interests
of the owner or tenant of shooting rights. The Game Laws are
so full of contradictions that it is inevitable that the laws protecting

L

the owners or tenants of shooting rights should be full of contradictions too. Both show all too many signs of ignorance and
haste.

The Game Act, 1831, did not inaugurate the era of game-bird
shooting in this country. Game-bird shooting and all other forms
of field sports, if not in quite the same form as at the present day,
had been going on in Great Britain and Ireland for many years.
The authors of the great classics of our sporting literature—Henry
Alken, William Daniel, John Colquhoun, Francis Fawkes, George
Hanger, Peter Hawker, Lawrence Rawstorne, Charles St. John,
William Scrope, Thomas Thornton—wrote before the passing of
the Act, or wrote of experiences enjoyed for the most part before
the passing of the Act. There were gamekeepers of a sort before
the passing of the Act. There were poachers before the passing
of the Act. But you will find that none of these classic authors
wastes much time on either gamekeepers or poachers. Colonel
George Hanger has some entertaining ideas on the subject of dealing
with poachers, centred around the firing of one of the pieces of
artillery which he had brought back from the Peninsular War
and erected in his grounds as a souvenir. Lawrence Rawstorne
evidently employed man-traps on his estate—he had humane ones,
and others described, briefly, as " large "—and three of his keepers
had pistols (one with a bayonet), but nowhere in his book does
Rawstorne discourse on poachers or their methods. Indeed,
speaking from memory, I do not think that he uses the word anywhere in his book. No; none of these classic authors shows any
concern about poachers and their activities. And this was not
because game-birds were not preserved, and in some cases artificially
reared, for they were. The whole of Lawrence Rawstorne's book,
Gamonia, is concerned with the preservation of game, and, especially,
of pheasants. It was published in 1837, six years after the passing
of the Game Act, but it is chiefly concerned with the years 1820–
1830. Nowhere in this book is the Game Act mentioned, which
means either that the book was completed before the Act was
passed and that the author did not think it important enough to
warrant any alteration in his book, or that the author had not heard
of the Act at all. I think that the latter is most improbable. Rawstorne would have heard of it, would almost certainly have known
all about it long before it reached the Statute Book. Much more
probable is it that Colonel Lawrence Rawstorne, English squire

of ancient lineage, regarded the Act with contempt and as of little importance and so ignored it.

For the Game Act was not passed because of the activities of poachers, because these activities had exceeded all abounds. It was passed as a result of the Enclosures. It was passed to strengthen the position of the landowner at the expense of the peasantry. That it brought a little money into the Treasury at the same time was a pleasant, but secondary, consideration. It was primarily a repressive measure. The Enclosures were not popular. They changed the whole of the basic economy of the nation, pauperising the peasantry, swallowing up much of the common lands and the rights that went with them, the while they enhanced the status and power of the landowner. No one had hitherto bothered very much about what was game and what was not. Sport was sport, and the peasant could enjoy his sport over the common lands if he so desired. Sport was sport to the wealthy landowner, too—you have only to read Rawstorne, Hawker and St. John to see that very clearly—and they took such steps as they thought necessary to protect their sport from undesirable and criminal elements. But no more than that. They did not interfere with the peasant's sport. Sport was sport until the Enclosures were well under way. Then sport became entangled with prestige (it has suffered ever since because of this) and, since it was now a matter of prestige, the peasant could no longer enjoy it. And then came another discovery: that, since it was a matter of prestige, there was money in it. Hence the Game Act of 1831, as ill-designed, ignorant and hurried a measure as one could well imagine. And one that is still (more or less) in force.

And all the other Acts designed to protect the interests of the owner of shooting rights, since they are based finally on the Game Act (*i.e.*, on the definition of what is game), suffer because of the inconsistencies and contradictions of the parent.

To begin with, all these Acts—read them and you will see that this is true—presuppose an ownership of game. But there is in the law of England and Scotland no property in game or in wild animals in their natural state. In Scotland they become the property of whoever captures them, even if in so doing the captor breaks the law, unless forfeiture of the game is made a part of the penalty for the offence. But in England (and Ireland) the law is much more complicated. In England if game is flushed and killed on the ground of one landowner it becomes his property (while it is alive it is the property of nobody), but if it is flushed on the ground of one man and killed on the ground of another, it becomes the property of the latter. (Consider the law of trespass in relation to boundaries, which I have dealt with briefly above, and you will find yet another contradiction.) This question of ground ownership and the place of flushing in relation to that of killing or capture has been put to good account on more than one occasion by poachers.

There are two further points that deserve special mention. While there is in law no property in game or wild animals, this does not include young game. Young game, unable to leave the nest or soil of its home, is the property of the owner of the soil. And tame animals or animals that have been tamed are the property of the person who keeps them. This covers young pheasants hatched from a sitting of eggs by a farmyard hen, for such young pheasants are considered to be tame for so long as they follow their foster-mother. To take them is theft, and is punishable as theft. But immediately they do leave their foster-mother, or, in the case of wild birds, immediately they leave the nest, the position changes. Dead game, by the way, does not come under any of the Game Laws. It is not a special offence to appropriate dead meat. And it is not theft to take game before it has become the property of someone—usually in this relation (but one can think of other possibilities!)—before it is killed or bagged. Thus a man walking along a public road while pheasants are being shot on the adjoining land may pick up a dead bird falling in the road and take it away. He is not guilty of theft, and he has not broken any of the Game Laws.

The Wild Birds' Protection Acts are quite different and separate from the Game Acts. Swans, geese, wild duck, teal, wigeon, all other ducks and capercaillie come under the provisions of the Wild Birds' Protection Acts for protection during the close seasons. So do other wild birds, including predatory birds. One of the ordinary duties of a gamekeeper is the destruction of vermin, which might destroy the game he is employed to preserve. In his case, obviously, predatory birds are classed as vermin. But his duty to his employer does not absolve him from obeying the law. It does not allow him to contravene the Wild Birds' Protection Acts.

These Acts contain five main provisions:

(1) That between 1st March and 1st August no one except the owner or occupier of the land, or persons authorised by him, may shoot, trap, snare, or otherwise destroy any wild bird.

(2) That during the same period certain birds named in a Schedule (some eighty different kinds) may not be taken or killed by *any one, including the owner or occupier of the land and the gamekeepers employed by him.*

(3) That this Schedule may be added to or varied (*i.e.*, the period of protection may be lengthened) in respect of particular counties.

(4) That the eggs of certain birds may be protected.

(5) That certain rare or useful birds shall be protected *throughout* the year *even from owners or occupiers of the land and their gamekeepers.*

Under the Wild Birds' Protection Acts some degree of protection is granted to the following predatory birds: the golden eagle, the white-tailed eagle, the peregrine falcon, the buzzard, the rough-legged buzzard, the kite, the sparrow-hawk, the kestrel, the osprey, the merlin, the hobby, the honey-buzzard, the marsh harrier, the hen harrier, Montagu's harrier, the raven, the carrion crow, the hooded crow, the rook, the jackdaw, the magpie, the jay, the brown owl, the barn owl, the long-eared owl, the short-eared owl, the little owl, the kittiwake, the great black-backed gull, the lesser black-backed gull, the common gull, the herring gull, the black-headed gull. The degree of protection varies with the county, and in a few counties a few of these birds (differing again from county to county) receive no protection.

Among the predatory birds absolutely protected—and absolute protection, you will remember, means protection from the owner or occupier of the land and the gamekeepers employed by him—*throughout* the year in certain counties are the following: the golden eagle, the white-tailed eagle, the peregrine falcon, the buzzard, the osprey, the kestrel, the rough-legged buzzard, the hen harrier, the marsh harrier, Montagu's harrier, the kite, the merlin, the hobby, the raven, the honey buzzard, the magpie, the kittiwake, the common gull, the herring gull, the black-headed gull, and all the owls except the little owl. The prevalent idea that the little owl is absolutely protected throughout the year in some counties is quite erroneous. It is protected throughout the year in some of the counties, but in no county does it receive absolute protection.

Among the predatory birds absolutely protected in some counties between the 1st March and the 1st August are the golden eagle, the peregrine falcon, the rough-legged buzzard, the honey buzzard, the buzzard, the kite, the osprey, the kestrel, the merlin, the marsh harrier, the hen harrier, Montagu's harrier, the raven, the magpie, the jay, the kittiwake, the common gull, the herring gull, the black-headed gull, and all the owls except the little owl.

Ordinary protection, it must be emphasised, includes protection from shooting tenants and the gamekeepers employed by them, unless the shooting tenant is also the occupier of the land. Thus, the little owl is in some counties protected throughout the year. In such counties the shooting tenant or his gamekeeper who shoots or otherwise destroys it is breaking the law. In some other counties the little owl is protected between 1st March and 1st August, in common with all other wild birds, and here again the shooting tenant or his gamekeeper who shoots or otherwise destroys it is breaking the law. The same applies to the sparrow-hawk and all the other predatory birds, except where a special by-law has been passed removing *all* protection. This has been done only in the case of the little owl, and then only in a few counties.

Summed up, this means that, except in those cases in which absolute protection has been granted, no wild bird may be shot or otherwise destroyed between 1st March and 1st August save by the owner or the occupier of the land or by persons properly authorised by him, and in certain counties this prohibition may apply throughout the year.

At first sight this seems definite enough. It is, of course, nothing of the sort. To take an extreme case: a bird may be absolutely protected throughout the year on one side of a hedge and receive no protection whatsoever on the other, and the land on each side of that hedge may be owned by the same man or occupied by the same man. In another case a bird is absolutely protected between 1st March and 1st August on one side of a hedge and only protected on the other. Again, the period of ordinary protection may vary on each side of a boundary. For example, in Devonshire the kite is protected absolutely throughout the year, while in Dorset it receives only ordinary protection between 1st March and 1st August. And again, in Hampshire the sparrow-hawk receives ordinary protection between 1st March and 1st August, while in Surrey it receives ordinary protection between 1st February and 31st August. In some cases this sort of thing becomes quite fantastic. Thus in East Suffolk the golden eagle is absolutely protected throughout the year, while in West Suffolk it receives only ordinary protection between 1st March and 1st August. In this county the same is true of a number of other birds, including the osprey, the raven, the merlin and the kite. Examples of this sort of thing occur all over the country.

The result of this extreme variation is that the law is so constantly broken that it has ceased to be observed at all. The chief offenders are the shooting men—owners, occupiers, tenants and gamekeepers—and egg-collectors. Very occasionally an egg-collector is caught, brought before the Justices, and fined £1 for each egg he has taken. Still more occasionally (I can recall only one case) a gamekeeper is caught, brought before the Justices, and, after a good deal of hesitation, fined. The maximum fine is £1 for each bird taken or killed. The maximum is usually imposed upon the egg-collectors; in the only case I can recall concerning a gamekeeper a reduced fine was imposed. I know of no case of an owner, an occupier or a shooting tenant being hauled before the Justices for an offence against the Wild Birds' Protection Acts. The guileless might think that, since there are no prosecutions, these gentlemen never break the laws. That is most definitely not the case. These laws are constantly broken, not by all, but by a very large number of shooting men (the large landowner of the old school—a type, unfortunately, rapidly becoming extinct—is a glorious exception, frequently providing sanctuary for birds that prey upon his game and enjoying doing so), but they are not prosecuted, although the whole neighbourhood usually knows all about it. The reason is not far to seek, and applies also in the case of gamekeepers. The owner or the occupier (and more often than not the shooting tenant) is almost certain to have friends on the Bench, and may be a Justice himself; and that applies to him as powerfully as the employer of an offending gamekeeper. It very rarely applies in the case of an egg-collector, for the man caught is usually a professional, serious egg-collectors preferring to employ others to do their work for them.

There is no excuse for any of these men, no excuse for the shooting man or for the egg-collector. Most of them can read. Both of them know well that they are breaking the law, and both try to justify themselves by stressing the sins of the others. It is a thoroughly undignified proceeding, which reflects little credit on either.

The egg-collector, who has been accused more than once of causing the disappearance of some of our rarest breeding birds, replies that they would breed if they were not shot at sight, and that in any case if he takes one clutch the bird will lay again, but that a dead bird cannot breed. There is a good deal of truth in that, especially where big birds are concerned. At the same time, some of the smaller birds, which are of no interest to the gamekeeper, would probably breed again in this country were it not for the egg-collectors. The latter's argument has some force only when it applies to the predatory birds. I think that there can be no doubt that the extinction of some of our larger predatory birds has been due to the excessive zeal (and ignorance) of gamekeepers, and I have no doubt that but for that zeal some of them would breed again. Indeed, that has been proved more than once during the recent war, and twice last year, in Hampshire, though in each case landowners of the old school took firm steps to ensure the safety of the rare predatory birds that nested. Rare predatory birds also nested during the war in other parts of England and Wales. It must be remembered, however, that during the war both game-keepers and egg-collectors were for the most part otherwise engaged, and it is almost certainly true to say that if a gamekeeper, on strict orders from his employer, allowed a pair of ospreys to breed, the egg-collectors would see to it that the eggs were never hatched.

The activities of the egg-collectors pass more or less unnoticed by the general public. Not so the activities of the shooting fraternity, and particularly the gamekeepers, for those people who are opposed to field sports, which they persist in calling blood sports or cruel sports, take good care to work up a case against them on the flimiest grounds. And this propaganda has produced a counter-stream of propaganda on behalf of those whose interest it is to further the activities of the gamekeeper.

The case for the gamekeeper and the shooting man is that it is necessary to keep in check furred and feathered vermin in order to preserve game, and that since feathered vermin prey indiscriminately upon game, poultry and song-birds, the gamekeeper, while performing the duties of his employment, is the man responsible for preserving the wonderful chorus of bird-song for which Britain is noted. In support of this contention it is pointed out that the National Trust, whose statutory duty includes the preservation of animal life, lets the shooting on certain of its properties in order to save the expense of keepering, since the preservation of animal life " calls for active steps to keep down the number of species which may prey too heavily on other species ". While it is true that gamekeepers are, indirectly, responsible for the preservation of a number of non-predatory birds, the gravamen of the charge against them as a class is that they have been responsible for the extermination of some of our rarer birds of prey, and for the constant breaking of the law in the killing that is considered an essential part of their duties.

That the gamekeeper has been responsible for the extermination, or virtual extermination, of some of our rarer birds of prey is indignantly denied. The egg-collector, say the supporters of the gamekeeper, is responsible for this, and the gamekeeper, they continue, is just the man to prevent egg-collectors from egg-collecting.

That the gamekeeper kills unnecessarily is also indignantly denied. He kills, say his supporters, only to protect his charges. He is, according to his supporters, a student. Some even go so far as to maintain that gamekeepers are good naturalists. A dead body is, however, irrefutable evidence, and they will admit that occasionally certain birds are shot in mistake for other species and in ignorance of the law protecting them.

Now, this case for the gamekeeper is easily destroyed. It will not stand a moment's investigation. Even the suggestion that the wealth of bird-song in Britain is due largely to his activities will not bear investigation. Was there less bird-song before there was game preservation? Is there less bird-song in those areas where so many migrant songsters breed and where there is no game preservation? (In fact, of course, song-bird population is not governed by the number of predators alone. Nor is the chief cause of extermination predators or egg-collecting or shooting. It is ecological: the draining of marshes, the building of roads and houses, and so forth—factors of enormous importance that are too frequently overlooked.) And, while it is perfectly true that the gamekeeper is just the man to prevent egg-collecting, and beyond doubt does prevent a certain amount in the case of rare non-predatory birds, it is difficult indeed to congratulate him in the case of rare predatory birds. A dead bird cannot lay eggs. What chance has an osprey, for instance, of breeding in England now? The bird is shot almost as soon as it is seen. That the gamekeeper kills only to protect his charges is certainly true. How much of the killing is necessary is another matter. But it is quite ridiculous to say that the gamekeeper is a student of nature or a good naturalist, and at the same time to admit that he sometimes kills certain birds in mistake for others. It is possible to do that, it is even easy to do that, in the heat of a drive. The gamekeeper does not work under those conditions. A good naturalist does not mistake species (for what can one mistake an osprey or a peregrine falcon?), and a student of nature would be the first to take pains to discover exactly the identity of the bird. Furthermore, a good naturalist would know sufficient of the habits of birds to know which were harmful and which were not, and a student of nature would very soon find out. The harriers and the buzzards, for example, do little or no damage to game, and they are not easily mistaken for other species. Yet they are shot often enough. And to say the gamekeeper may sometimes shoot a bird in ignorance of the fact that it is protected by the law is no defence and no excuse. He should know the law. It is all there in black and white at the local police-station.

But though it is all too easy to demolish the case put forward for the gamekeeper, and though there is absolutely no excuse for the gamekeeper not knowing the law, since from the very nature of his employment he should be at pains to know the law, it would be grossly unfair to blame him for breaking the law. He is paid to do a certain job. His livelihood depends upon his doing that job to the satisfaction of his employer. The man upon whom the blame must rest in those cases in which the law is broken is the employer.

Where the employer is both the owner of the land and a naturalist or a lover of birds and wild life (and a man can be those things and a sportsman: the best of both is a combination of both), the law is not broken, and rare birds of prey are not destroyed, and the shooting is not spoilt. Indeed, so far from being destroyed in such cases, they are protected. A case in point is that of the late Lord Desborough and his head-keeper, the late Jim Vincent—

great sportsmen and great naturalists both. There are, fortunately, many other cases. And in these cases not only are the laws observed and rare birds protected, but the egg-collector is defeated and the shooting does not suffer. In Hampshire recently the hen harrier and Montagu's harrier and the buzzard have all bred success-fully in a district that is famed for its game preservation. The birds were protected on the strict orders of the three landowners concerned, all very keen shooting men, and the shooting did not suffer at all, and the gamekeepers concerned were delighted at their success. If this can happen in one place, in several places, it can happen in others. It could happen everywhere.

But it will not happen everywhere. It will probably, with the growth of the syndicate shoot, happen less frequently in the future. The gamekeeper will be blamed. But it will not be his fault at all. It will not happen partly because so many shooting tenants are men with no roots in the country (and their number is going to increase), but chiefly because of the law itself. The Wild Birds' Protection Acts are so numerous, so various and so contradictory that they have come to be completely ignored. To all intents and purposes they are a dead letter. It is the earnest, but ignorant, framers of the laws who must bear the blame.

And one further word in favour of the gamekeeper. I know a great many gamekeepers. And I have met them under all sorts of circumstances: as member of shooting-parties, as member of Gypsy parties, as the editor of a newspaper, as common or garden trespasser, and so on. I have probably seen them at work from more angles than any other man in the country—from both sides of the fence, as it were—and I have the greatest admiration for them. They are as a whole a very fine body of men, and they do not receive the recognition that is their due. While I know few whom I could truthfully call good naturalists, I know very few indeed whom I could truthfully accuse of killing for killing's sake, or even of killing, in view of the nature of their employment and, more particularly, of their employers, unnecessarily. Unfortu-nately, I cannot say as much for many shooting men I know. Year after year I get birds sent to me for identification, birds absolutely protected by law; birds shot by men who should know better; birds shot because the man behind the gun did not know what they were and wanted to find out; birds shot, so their killers say, in mistake for other species. For example, a bittern shot in mistake for a goose! an osprey shot in mistake for a sparrow-hawk!—actual cases those that have come to my table in the past two years, and both shot by educated men.

This sort of thing is not unnaturally eagerly seized upon by those who wish to have shooting (among other field sports) abolished. They make considerable capital out of it—the " lust for blood ", " killing for killing's sake ", and so on—and, as good propagandists, they make it appear that it is the common practice throughout the shooting world. Never by any chance do they mention those shooting men by whose disinterested protection a number of rare birds have been brought back as breeding species to Britain.

But more important than the propaganda of the anti-sport bodies (for propaganda has invariably a boomerang effect), and far more dangerous than any anti-sport movement for the future of shooting, is the disgust these thoughtless actions arouse among those who are not anti-sport, but who do love birds and are not interested in the pheasant, the partridge and the grouse to the exclusion of all others, among naturalists and bird-lovers generally. Such people, I find, are very inclined to blame gamekeepers and to regard all gamekeepers as men anxious to kill anything with a hooked beak. They are inclined to regard all shooting men as supremely selfish. And they do not give sufficient credit, perhaps because they have not heard of them, to those shooting men and landowners who are the best protectionists in the country. It is due entirely to the unselfish protection of shooting men that that noble predator, the golden eagle—a bird that does a good deal of harm on a grouse moor— is in so strong a position to-day. The harriers would not have come back to Hampshire and Norfolk if it had not been for the shooting men in counties famous for their shooting. But you cannot blame the bird-lover. After all, it is ninety-nine times out of a hundred the shooting man who shoots a rare bird and then writes to the papers about it. That among the vast number of men who shoot these light-fingered gentry form a comparatively small proportion is not realised, nor is it realised that their activities are deplored, genuinely deplored, by the best type of shooting man.

The British Field Sports Society does everything it can to educate those who shoot to a due sense of their responsibilities. And it has recently published a booklet setting out the measures of protection granted to each of the predatory birds in each of the counties. It is very clearly done, and it is very well illustrated. There will in future be remarkably little excuse for the shooting man or the game-keeper who "mistakes" an osprey for a sparrow-hawk, or who kills a hawk or a falcon or a harrier merely because it has a hooked beak, and then pleads ignorance of the law. Conversely, of course, the more these birds are shot in the future in defiance of the law, the stronger will be the case of the bird-lover and the more shrill will be the war-cry (shriek is a more accurate description) of the anti-sport fanatic.

But when all that has been said, when all the good work of the British Field Sports Society has been taken into account, when all the excellent protective work of certain landowners and their game-keepers has been acknowledged and set forth as an example, we come back to the law. A law that cannot be enforced will not be respected. Neither the Game Laws nor the Wild Birds' Protection Acts can be enforced. That, bluntly, is the position. That the Game Laws are enforced occasionally is true, but they are enforced only against those who have no position or privilege in the district. The same is true of the Wild Birds' Protection Acts. Both sets of laws are broken every day, and most countrymen know that they are broken and when they are broken and by whom they are broken, for the average countryman is by no means ignorant of the laws affecting wild life, no matter what he may pretend. The man who breaks the law is not respected by those who do not. And the man who breaks the law and is heavily fined or sent to prison for doing so has nothing but contempt for the Bench that punishes him, when he knows, as he does, that it is lenient to the privileged wrong-doer.

Contempt for the law and for those who are supposed to ad-minister it is a dangerous thing. It is high time that the Game Laws were brought up to-date, and the Wild Birds' Protection Acts were rationalised.

Epilogue

THE OLDEN DAYS

FOR comparison I give here three extracts from *The Gentleman's Recreation*, which was written by Richard Blome and published in 1686. The title of this book is especially worthy of note.

A WAY TO TAKE PIGEONS, ROOKS, OR CROWS, VERY PLEASANT.

Take some thick *Brown-Paper*, cut a Sheet into about 8 parts, and make them up like *Sugar Loaves*, then *Lime* the inside of the *Paper* indifferent well three or four days before you intend to set them ; then put into each *Paper*, towards the further end, two or three Grains of *Corn*, lay these papers up and down the *Ground*, and as near as you can under some *Clods* of *Earth*, early in the *Morning* before they come to *feed* : for the quantity you may use your discretion, the more the better, about a hundred is indifferent. When they come to feed they will espy the *Corn*, and begin to peck them out by thrusting in their *Heads* ; then they are hoodwinked, for they can't get it off by reason it sticks so close to their *Feathers* ; when they find themselves thus served they take Wing, and will fly bolt-upright until they have spent themselves ; and then come tumbling down to the delight of the Spectators.

TO TAKE WATERFOWL.

Take the *Seeds*, *Leaves*, and *Roots* of the herb called *BELLENGE*, and having cleansed them from all filth, put them into a *Vessel* of clean *Running-Water*, and let them lie sleeping therein at least twenty-four *hours*, and then boyl them in the said *water* until it is almost consumed ; then take it off the *fire*, let it cool, and scatter it in such places where the *Fowl* have their *haunts* ; they will greedily eat it, so that they become immediately intoxicated, and lie in a Trance as if dead ; but you must watch them, for the Fumes will soon wear off.

Some do add to this Concoction the Powder of *BRIMSTONE*, boiled therein, which is very effectual.

TO TAKE LANDFOWL.

Take a Peck, or a lesser quantity of *Wheat*, *Rye*, *Barley*, *Pease*, or *Tares*, to which put two or three handfuls of *NUX-VOMICA*, and boyl them in *Running-Water* very well, until they are almost

174

ready to burst ; then take it off the *Fire*, and when they are cold strew them upon the *land* where you design to take the *Fowl*, and such as eat thereof will immediately be intoxicated, and lye as if dead ; so that you may take them up at pleasure, provided you stay not too long (for the dizziness will not last long upon them, therefore be near at hand).

If you approve not of *NUX-VOMICA* you may boil the said *Grains* or *Seeds* in the *Lees* of *Wine* (the stronger the better). . . .

Or instead of the *NUX-VOMICA*, or *LEES* of *WINE*, you may infuse the said *Grains* or *Seeds* in the Juice of Hemlock, mixing therein the *Seeds* of *Henbane* and *Poppy* or either of them.